# GRIEVING THE DEATH OF A MOTHER

## Harold Ivan Smith

**Augsburg Books**
MINNEAPOLIS

IN MEMORY OF MY MOTHER

MARY CATHERINE ECKERT SMITH

APRIL 2, 1916–FEBRUARY 21, 1999

GRIEVING THE DEATH OF A MOTHER

Large-quantity purchases or custom editions of this book are available at a discount from the publisher. For more information, contact the sales department at Augsburg Fortress, Publishers, 1-800-328-4648, or write to: Sales Director, Augsburg Fortress, Publishers, P.O. Box 1209, Minneapolis, MN 55440-1209.

Scripture passages are from the New Revised Standard Version of the Bible, copyright © 1946, 1952, 1971, 1989 by the Division of Christian Education of the National Council of the Churches of Christ in the USA. Used by permission.

*Library of Congress Cataloging-in-Publication Data*
Smith, Harold Ivan, 1947-
  Grieving the death of a mother / Harold Ivan Smith.
      p. cm.
Includes bibliographical references.
  ISBN 0-8066-4347-1
  1. Grief. 2. Bereavement—Psychological aspects. 3. Mothers—Death—Psychological aspects. 4. Loss (Psychology) I. Title.

BF575.G7S593 2003
155.9'37—dc21                                       2002154922

Cover design by Mira Skocka; original cover art by Mira Skocka
Book design by Michelle L. N. Cook

The paper used in this publication meets the minimum requirements of American National Standard for Information Sciences—Permanence of Paper for Printed Library Materials, ANSI Z329.48-1984. ♾ ™

Manufactured in the U.S.A.

07     06     05     04     03     1     2     3     4     5     6     7     8     9     10

# CONTENTS

# INTRODUCTION

*Sometimes I feel like a motherless child. . . . A long way from home.*
  —African American spiritual

*My mother died recently, and suddenly I wanted to go home and be a child again.*
  —Laura Scott[1]

*I miss being someone's daughter. . . . So now I go through life with one less person keeping an eye on me, one less person loving me.*
  —Joyce Maynard[2]

*I am again a traveler, wandering through a landscape for which Fodor has no guidebook—a land called Grief.*
  —Harold Ivan Smith[3]

A MOTHER'S DEATH CAN MAKE SHAMBLES of schedules, priorities, agendas, commitments—sometimes, our most intimate relationships. A mother's last breath inevitably changes us. Motherlessness can be paralyzing or it can be empowering. It can cause us to take life far more seriously. I know. My mother died on February 21, 1999.

As a grief educator, I thought I was prepared for my mother's death. After all, I help people deal with the death of their mothers. I had no idea one death could continuously ricochet down the corridors of a heart.

> Grief for a mother will have its days—
> sometimes long after the rituals are over and
> condolence cards have stopped coming in the mail.
> Whenever I am convinced that grief is "done"
> Bang! It's back! As if there is an
> invisible bungee chord that pulls me back to my grief.
> There is—memory.

My mother's guidance throughout my childhood can be summarized by her continual admonition: "Now, I want you to be a big boy." Trying to be a big boy during my mother's dying and at her visitation, funeral, and committal proved challenging. It was as if death had ambushed me: "You know very little, Mister!" It was as if a menacing drill instructor had commandeered my heart.

As a grief educator, I encourage thorough grief. No "light" grief, no short cuts, and no time off for good behavior; the day-in, day-out work of grief is necessary and important. Unfortunately, I grieve in a society that aggressively limits grief, that reprimands, "You should be over your mother's death by now" (sometimes punctuated with an exclamation point). It's as if a game clock somewhere determines how much grief time one gets.

After my mother's funeral, I frequently felt as though I had run a gauntlet of questions: "How old was your mother?" When I answered eighty-three, the frequent response was, "Oh, then she lived a good long life." "Oh" felt like a slap to my face. What would have been wrong with her living eighty-four or eighty-eight years? "Was she a Christian?" Yes. "Well, then, she's in a better place." "Had she been sick?" Yes. "Then her suffering is over." Yes, but what about *my* suffering? Grief, particularly for an aged mother, is disenfranchised. Jeanine Cannon Bozeman writes: "I perceived that many people felt that because mother was 'old,' and I was an adult child, the loss should be less significant."[4]

> It does not matter who you are or how high
> or low your status in society:
> how old or young you are
> how experienced you are in the black-and-blue realities of life
> how clever you are with words
> losing a mother wounds.

For the rest of life, some will have great difficulty finding words to wrap around a mother's death. A song, a scent, a taste, a fabric, or a memory will leave us wordless.

It does not matter how self-confident you are—losing a mother deprives you of a chief cheerleader. A friend once told me: "I lost the one person who would love me no matter what happened in my life. I always knew my mother would be there for me." "What about your husband?" I protested. Without hesitation, she replied, "Like I said, 'I lost the one person who would love me no matter what happened in my life.'" Some have lost mothers at an early age; others have never known their mothers. Some have lost mothers through abandonment, custody battles, mental illness, addictions, dementia, Alzheimer's, and then through death. Those who mourn motherloss know the deep reality found in the words to the African American spiritual "Sometimes I feel like a motherless child." Long after the rituals, the words of this spiritual take on new meaning. Many have lost mothers without warning through automobile accidents, heart attacks, murders, or suicides. Many grievers are left burdened with unfinished business, apologies that were never verbalized, unexpressed appreciations, and unspoken affections. My friend Carl captured the feelings of many when he said, "I still needed her. I wasn't finished growing up yet."

Some have witnessed a slow, agonizing death that has left them whimpering for grace or shaking a fist at a God who could allow such cruelty or injustice. Will I ever forget the first time I found my mother in diapers? Or the first time my mother did not know me?

Me! Her baby, Harold Ivan! Some have lost mothers while trying to survive other life crises: downsizing, divorce, our own illness, the death of a child. The one we would have turned to is no longer there to comfort us. After a mother dies, any crisis feels more menacing. A mother might not have known what to say or do, but she would have listened to the end of our sentences, even the ones that rambled incoherently.

Some mothers served as the glue that held a fragile family together. Some of us grieve for a mother *and* for a family that disintegrated after her death. Some siblings have been on their best behavior while their mother was dying. Nothing—including family dysfunction—was allowed to upset mother. That fragile truce continued in some families through the rituals; in others, all it took to unravel was divvying up mom's estate. A punch bowl can become a battleground that resurrects old family issues. The family has never been the same—and never will be. Family histories may be divided BMD and AMD: *before* Mom's death and *after* Mom's death.

Motherloss is heightened by the annual emphasis with motherhood on the second Sunday in May. Mother's Day was started by Anna Jarvis as she experienced deep grief for her mother, who died in 1905. Merchants have dozens of ways to remind you that it's Mother's Day. Hope Edelman says, "I'm still trying to figure out how to revise the Roman calendar and leapfrog straight from April to June" to avoid Mother's Day.[5] But other red-letter days can sharply remind us that mother is dead, such as Thanksgiving, Christmas, Kwanza, Valentine's Day, or even the Fourth of July, when Mom's baked beans or devil's food cake was the highlight of a picnic or backyard barbecue. Holidays are different after a mother dies.

Even Christmas carols can ambush us. How many times have I wiped away tears when hearing "Silent Night"? How many times have I tried to force the words of my mother's beloved carols past the lump in my throat? Just now, sitting in a library editing this manuscript, I bite my lip to stop the tears that are forming as I remember mother singing "O Holy Night, the stars are brightly shining. . . ." I can be in a crowded mall and hear those words over all the racket and clamor of holiday shoppers and remember.

Grievers are reminded of their loss by the birthday card not received or sent; a present not given or received; a missed regular phone call; a taken-to-the-grave favorite recipe.

To avoid the pain, some grievers make an unspoken collusion: Do not mention Mother. Fergus Bordewich, whose mother died in a horse-riding accident when he was fourteen years old, captured the experience of many: "My father and I almost never talked about my mother or what had happened in Vermont."[6] Fergus experienced lonely evenings spent with his father watching *Gunsmoke* or *Bonanza* "separated by a space that neither of us had any idea how to bridge. Each of us had learned by now not to ask questions, to mind his own business, to maneuver around the other's silences."[7] Many grievers spend days and nights maneuvering around the questions. Like survivors in a war zone, we become accomplished at dodging emotional land mines.

I miss my mom's house. I miss home. I miss walking in the back door and smelling something fresh from the oven and Mom hugging me, "Oh, I'm glad you're home. . . . Have you had anything to eat?" No one was ever underfed under my mom's roof. Phrases such as "It will only take a minute" and "It's no trouble at all" were always on her lips. I miss my bedroom. I miss the closet filled with childhood toys and memorabilia.

The house at 4809 Beech Drive was sold to settle the estate. New owners moved in, and I received a check. Initially, I could not deposit the check. That transaction would finalize my mother's death. Ironically, the day I deposited the check, in the normal chitchat of doing business, I discovered that my banker's mother had just died. We both experienced an "Ah, someone understands" moment. We continued to talk while other customers waited. A soul transaction was underway.

The mood was shaken by a mistake. The banker had entered in too many zeroes. For ninety seconds, I was a millionaire—at least on the computer screen—until she caught the mistake. I am sure that in heaven my mother laughed and grabbed someone to say, "My son's a millionaire!"

Motherloss has a way of sneaking into any activity and saying, "Tag. You're it." As I write these words, I am closely observing a young family playing a table game. Not that many years ago, I too was a young boy at a table wanting my mother's attention. Do these two young teens have any idea how much they will eventually miss such moments with their mother? Can anyone comprehend this before her death? I want to whisper: "Guys, pay attention. Look at your mother. Listen to her. Memorize this moment. Someday this memory will comfort you—or confront you."

The missing and mourning do not go away on any timetable acceptable to our rushed society. How many times did Mom ask, "What's the big hurry?" This is why someone's challenge, "Isn't it time you move on?" resounds. The word *still* functions like a scouring pad. "You're still grieving for your mother!" I marvel that more people are not beaten severely about the head and shoulders for questioning a timetable of grief. (Most are too polite to defend our right to grieve.)

Although I am fifty-four years old, I still need my mom. I am not "all grown up." Just once more I would like to hear, "Oh, I am so glad you called. I was just thinking about you. Did you have something good to eat today?"

In those moments when my life and dreams caved in, my mom was always a phone call away. My mom promised that there would be blue skies when I could only imagine perpetual gray. My mother was always able to tell when I was stressed. It seemed as though she always concluded our phone conversations the same way: "Oh, Honey, it will work out someway. Just don't worry about it. You hear?" What I would give for one of those phone calls today.

What do I miss about my mother? Innumerable things. I miss my mother's words at Christmas, Mother's Day, and on her birthdays: "Honey, I wish you hadn't spent your money on me." It was always the best money I spent in a year.

I miss opening a letter and finding a folded five-dollar bill. I miss her advice, "Be sure you bundle up before you jog." It didn't matter that I was thirty-two, forty-two, or fifty-two years old; to her, I was still her youngest child. I miss her pride in me and in my career. I had no idea that she had saved every postcard I had sent her in my travels around the world. To me, it was just a postcard; to my mother, it was a document as important as any school report card.

I miss her intuition that something was wrong. On one occasion, my mother knew that I was working in Haiti. So, when CNN reported "bloodshed in the streets of Port-of-Prince," she sat paralyzed for three days in front of the television, convinced that one of the bodies in the street could be me. I will never forget calling her and hearing an ecstatic, "It's you! Oh, Honey, I was so afraid that something bad had happened to you!" Now, no one worries about me. After all, I am a big boy. The world is scarier without a mom actively worrying and aggressively praying.

I miss her listening to my stories. Some stories never get told (or I tell the short version) because no one listens as thoroughly as a mother does.

After the initial mourning period has worn off—about thirty days—rarely does anyone say, "Tell me about your mother." I would often hear a mumbled, "Sorry to hear about your mother" or some variation thereof. But to know me, you would have to know Mary Catherine Eckert Smith.

The death of a mother creates a demanding learning curve. The psalmist's poetic phrase, "Tho I walk through the valley of the shadow of death" sounds different in my ear and heart. Things look different after you have buried your mother, after this shadow shines across your path and across your memories.

Amazingly, your brain logs in the fact of your mother's death, but it takes a long time for your heart to absorb the reality. There will be times when you pick up the phone to call, only to remember after the third digit. In a card shop you will be looking for just the right card, and then it will hit you.

Somehow *Grieving the Death of a Mother* has come to you—perhaps as a gift, or after someone has scribbled the title on a piece of paper and said, "Read this!" Perhaps you stumbled upon it while browsing through the grief section in the library or a bookstore. Maybe someone who does not know what to say has given it to you. You may have had the book for some time but are just now getting around to reading it.

I have been amazed by the number of people who, upon learning I was writing this book, have remarked, "I can't even think about losing my mother. I don't know what I will do when . . ." Well, sooner or later, life will make you think about motherloss— *your* motherloss. Because unless you die first, you are going to experience the death of a mother.

Make no mistake—the death of a mother can be one of life's toughest experiences. Ask George Herbert Walker Bush, Dwight Eisenhower, or Harry Truman—leaders of the free world, but nonetheless sons grieving for mothers who had uniquely nurtured them. Imagine the world's most powerful leader reduced to alternating tears and laughter, so much so that George Bush feared the reaction of his Secret Service detail. Dorothy Walker Bush died two weeks after he was defeated for reelection in 1992. He wrote in his diary:

> Mum left us. It's kind of like our compass is spinning a little. Even when she was tired and failing she was our guide. I walked up by the Bungalow a lot this long Thanksgiving weekend. I found myself choking up. Then I found myself smiling. The agents probably said to each other, "The old guy's finally lost it."[8]

Margaret Truman observed her father's long grief after her grandmother's death in 1947. Facing a tough reelection campaign, Truman missed his mother. "Mamma Truman's death removed from Dad's life the other woman [along with Bess Truman, his wife] to whom he had turned again and again for the emotional support he needed to maintain his balance in the presidency."[9] Eleven years after Martha Truman's death, Truman wrote Dean Atchison, who had served as his secretary of state, upon the death of Atchison's mother:

> I'll never forget my experience in 1947. So you may well know that my sympathy is heartfelt. There is no supporter like your

mother. Right or wrong from her viewpoint you are always right. She may scold you for little things, but never for the big ones.[10]

As I read Truman's letters in the Truman Presidential Library, I reminded myself: This mourning son was the President of the United States.

Remembrances of a mother ambush the griever in the most unlikely moments. Wrapping Christmas presents, I noticed that I am using my mother's scissors—my mother's "good" scissors. How many presents over the years had been wrapped with paper and ribbon cut with these scissors? Rather than snarl "Scat!" at the memories clamoring for my attention, I allowed myself an "I miss my mother" moment. Thorough grief makes ample room for dancing with the memories.

Make no mistake—your mother's death affects you regardless of the status of your relationship with her at the time of death. In ways apparent and not so apparent, motherloss shapes you. Elizabeth Hutchinson Jackson died of typhus in 1781 leaving a thirteen-year-old son, Andrew. A biographer writes:

> Betty had been the most important person in her son's life—the person who had advised him, admired him, believed in him, encouraged him, protected him against enemies. No one else . . . could fill those roles. He would revere her memory and cite her as an authority as long as he lived. Certain consequences of her death radiated through the rest of [Andrew] Jackson's life. The reverence he felt for his mother he would extend to women in general.[11]

If Mrs. Jackson had not died when Andrew was thirteen, would he have become the Andrew Jackson of destiny? Did loss shape his destiny? Millions around the world wondered what would happen to Prince William and Prince Harry when Princess Diana died. How many times have the media tackled the question, "How are Diana's sons doing?" Today, in every language of humankind, that question will be asked of children following a mother's death.

My mother and my grandmother were quilters. But before they would start quilting, the two of them figured out a quilt design—trying fabric pieces, tentatively making some choices, and fitting pieces together with straight pins. In *Grieving the Death of a Mother,* I will piece glimpses from my personal recollections of loss with recollections of individuals who have experienced the death of a mother. Hawaiians call the process *humuhumu*—fitting the pieces together.

A story, a sentence, perhaps a phrase, in these pages may be a "fit" with your experience of motherloss. The words of others will come alive for you and call upon your memories.

There will be moments while reading this book when you need to put it down and listen to your own heart, when you will need to *humuhumu*—fit some pieces together. There will be moments while reading when you will need to take a piece of paper or sit at a computer and let your words "loose." There will be moments while reading when you will need to walk or journal or pick up a crayon and draw.

Honor the moment. Honor your personal memories. Rehearse your stories that begin, "I will never forget the time my mother . . ." Close your eyes and revisit the moments of affirmation, the places and spaces of life. Audit your life for the telltale life prints of the one you called "Mother." Never apologize for your grief. The author of Ecclesiastes tell us that there is a time to mourn, a time to grieve (3:4). Embrace your grief. Work with it. Learn from it. By doing so, you honor your mother. By doing so, you model healthy grief and you give others permission to download their grief.

Victoria Alexander believed that every griever has three needs:

To find the words for the loss
To say the words aloud, and
To know that the words have been heard.[12]

May these words ignite your pursuit of the words. Give your grief its voice.

# A Prayer

Lord,
use the words, stories, and memories of others
who have lost mothers
to prompt my words, stories, and memories.
Give me courage to own my loss
and to grieve well.

# 1. THE DYING

*With human relationships, nothing is ever final.*
 —Laura Davis[1]

*Then she slipped away during the night, and I felt my anchor to the world tear loose. My whole life got ripped up as Mama's spirit eased itself out of our house. You just feel that your Mama will always be close by, to help you on your hard days and remind you of the truth when your mind and soul are confused. But Mama was gone, and I couldn't believe the Lord would do such a damaging thing. I was thirty-six.*
 —Venita Wright[2]

*You lose your history, your sense of connection to the past. You also lose the final buffer between you and death. Even if you're an adult, it's weird to be orphaned.*
 —Therese Rando[3]

IS THERE A CLEAR MOMENT THAT YOU CAN SAY "MY mother is dying?" The phrase "is dying" can echo brutally along the canyons of a child's heart; many are reluctant to verbalize the words. Some have been outraged to learn of a mother's death: "No one told me she was *dying*!" Some refuse to hear the diagnosis. Some thought their mother had nine lives; she had beaten other diagnoses, surely she would conquer this one, too. Mom is invincible!

In one sense, we are dying the moment we take our first breath, and we are living until we take our last breath. Some daughters and sons say the words "is dying" so softly in conversations one can hardly hear it. In other families, the reality is never acknowledged.

> Ask me, Sudden death or lingering suffering?
> Tonight I'll take "didn't know what hit her!"
> Tomorrow I'll rethink it.
> I can't think rationally
> > I'm too weary
> > I'm too emotionally unsettled
> > > by my inability to do anything
> > > other than sit here
> > > waiting for something to happen.

## The Beginning of the Ending

Some readers can identify with Malcolm Boyd's experience: "Years passed when I took my mother's good health and sense of security for granted. How was I to know that a sudden crisis would shatter this condition and well-being?" At the moment the ambulance backed down the driveway, Beatrice Boyd was not dying but, in her son's mind, "it became clear that she would never see her house again."[4] It was another mile marker on a death path. All of us know our mothers will die—none of us believe it.

I watched my mother die. As I watched her suffer, I agonized. I composed prayers that I could not have imagined uttering. Late one night, I scribbled a prayer of petition for my mother's death. I could not stand to witness such suffering.

Lord, take my mother, please!
Take her to be with you and Dad.
End her pain now!
Jesus, you never had to watch your mother die.
    What I am witnessing
    is enough to soften the heart
    of the hardest-hearted son.
Give her a boarding pass.

I felt overwhelmed with guilt! I had prayed for my mother to die. After some dark moments, I reminded myself that I had prayed for the suffering to end. Death was the only way her suffering could end.

The end began with a physical and mental evaluation of my mother. Clearly, she could not live by herself. The first stop was Rose Anna Hughes, an assisted-living facility—a challenge for my mother. After decades of living in her own home, sharing a small room and a bathroom with strangers was demanding if not demeaning. The first time I walked into her room I thought, "This isn't my mother. I've mixed up the room numbers." Then for some reason I called out, "Mom?"

"Oh, is that you, Honey?" The voice had not changed. I was in my mother's room. How could she have changed so dramatically since the last time I had seen her? I would have walked past her in a hallway. That was only the beginning of my walk in the long shadowed valley. Soon there would be complications from a broken hip, and skirmishes with incompetent administrators and staff, including one who knocked my mother down because she wasn't walking fast enough. I will never forget finding my mother lying naked on her bed, the door to the hall wide open. The nursing assistant did not have everything she needed to change her, so she had left Mom exposed.

I was outraged. "I want the administrator here now!" I bellowed. When a nurse's aide asked what was wrong, another "Now!" convinced her to find an administrator. I telephoned my sister. "I am at the nursing home. Mom is laying here stark naked and no one is around!" A few minutes later my sister arrived. Like tag-team wrestlers on cable TV, we demanded immediate change in mother's care.

> My mother had always been modest.
> To find her naked and dependent
> on the kindness of poorly paid strangers
> was an emotional tsunami which repeatedly
> slammed the shoreline of my heart.

Soon an administrator arrived. My mother was changed, clothed, and sitting on her bed. How do you have a conversation about what just happened? I knew that she knew. I also knew that I could not guarantee that it would never happen again.

Having had three years to reflect on Mom's dying, I envied Fergus Bordewich's experience: "I was grateful in a way that I had never seen her grow old, never seen her eyes dull, her flesh sag, her memory disintegrate, her optimism falter."[5] I had seen more than a son should ever see.

Then came that God-awful day when my mother waited in agitation for an aide to come take her to the bathroom. Wanting to calm her, I began reading Bible verses she had long appreciated. She pressed the call button repeatedly, her eyes darting from me to the doorway as I read from Lamentations: "The steadfast love of the Lord never ceases, his mercies never come to an end; they are new every morning; great is your faithfulness" (3:22-23).

My mother whispered, "We used to sing a song about that."

"Yes, Mom, we did. 'Great Is Thy Faithfulness.'" I began singing and soon she joined me.

> Great is thy faithfulness,
> Great is thy faithfulness,
> Morning by morning new mercies I see.
> All I have needed Thy hand has provided
> Great is Thy faithfulness, Lord unto me.[6]

As Mother began the second verse, I became aware that she had not been able to hold her bowels. While she filled her diaper, we sang about God's faithfulness. Eventually an aide came and changed my mother. My mother knew that I knew she had dirtied her diaper. Another piece of her fragile dignity had been stripped away.

Later in the parking lot I screamed at God. "Faithfulness! She is sitting there filling her diapers and yet she is singing about your 'faithfulness' to her! What kind of life is this?"

Throughout lunch I struggled with the morning's events. Yet, the real sandpaper on my heart was fear that someday I may sit dirtying myself in a nursing facility. Only there will not be a son sitting with me reading Lamentations or singing about the faithfulness of God. Watching a mother die can stir up anguishing fears and fantasies. Reeve Lindbergh writes:

> Looking in the morning mirror, I ask myself, What is that face that I see? How did I get here from childhood? A fifty-four-year-old woman with glasses and wrinkles, brooding about her confused ninety-three-year-old mother in diapers. This is not what I asked for! This is not where I wanted to be.[7]

## WHEN YOUR MAMA DOESN'T KNOW YOU

Recently, while double-checking a citation for this book, I happened upon a biography of Queen Victoria and discovered that the most powerful woman in the world had a similar experience with her mother, the Duchess of Kent. Although an attendant tried to comfort her, saying, "The end will be easy," Victoria was distraught.

> I knelt before her, kissed her dear hand and placed it next to my cheek; but though she opened her eyes, she did not, I think, know me. She brushed my hand off, and the dreadful reality was before me, that for the first time she did not know the child she had ever received with such tender smiles. . . . I went out to sob.[8]

If Victoria could sob, so could I. I and so many others have experienced, in Queen Victoria's words, "the dreadful reality."

I had flown into Louisville to speak in a nearby community, and decided to drop in at the nursing facility. I had concluded that dropping in would keep the personnel "on their toes." After that first tense encounter, one administrator frequently asked my sister, "When is your brother from Kansas City coming?"

I walked into my mother's room and said a cheery, "Hello, Mom" and hugged her. For a long time she studied me. I surmised that she did not know me.

"Have any of your children been to see you?" I asked. She pondered the question before answering yes. "How many children do you have?" "Two," she answered. (She had three.) "Have they been to see you today?" (I wanted to ask, "Do you know who I am?" but, if she did know, that directness would have embarrassed her. "Of course I know who you are!")

"What about your other son? Does he come to visit you?" "Sometimes," mother answered. She looked at me for quite a while as I commented on her room. Then she slung the zinger question: "Who are you?"

I laughed. "I am your son, Harold Ivan." Mom weighed the answer.

"Does that mean you're a Smith?"

I visited a while then explained that I had to leave.

"Will you come back and see me sometime?"

"Yes," I said, hugging her. "I will come back and see you on Sunday. In two days."

I drove to the motel and checked in. I pulled the curtains shut in the room and stretched out on the bed. A brief encounter with reality had walloped my heart. In just a few hours I was to speak at a conference and dazzle the participants. How could I do that? I had known, sooner or later, this day would come.

I had hoped for a nap but was too agitated. Later as I showered I reminded myself that "the show must go on." The audience had not come to hear me talk about my anguish. So, I just flipped a switch and did my thing. We all have to flip that switch at some point, just to make it through. After returning to the room, late into that night, I struggled with my grief. What I had feared has come upon me. My mother no longer knew me.

## SPEAKING THE TRUTH IN LOVE

Barbara Bartocci's mom was having a surgical implant and Barbara assumed that she understood the motivation for the procedure. As Barbara walked into the room just before surgery, however, her mother's eyes "were black with terror. She was, in that moment, a terrified child whose bony hand clasped mine." She plied Barbara with questions. The terror stunned her daughter. "How could this be my mother? My mother was never afraid." How many times had Mom quieted Barbara's fears as a child?

"I can't have this tube in me! How will I go to luncheon with my friends?" Barbara tried to quiet the fear but her mother persisted. "How long will I have this in? For five years? I'm not going to stand for something like this for five years!"

Barbara would long remember the moment that called for brutal honesty. "'Mom, you don't have five years, you know.' Her face grew whiter than white. She turned to the wall. I buried my own face in my hands. I had spoken a truth she didn't want to hear."[9]

We need to speak the truth in love. Some siblings avoid the truth of the dying. Some dodge reality with spiritual language: "Oh, we're trusting God for a miracle. . . ." We knew in Mom's case that her God was not planning a miracle. Some delay the dying, demanding that every procedure be used—never acknowledging that the high-tech medicine can only postpone the inevitable and, at times, increase the suffering for the dying and for those who wait.

## THE CONVERSATION WE NEVER HAD

Mary Jensen was stunned by the sight of her mother shuffling along an airport corridor. "She looked like someone else's elderly mother. . . . For the first time in my life she was fragile, porcelain, opalescent." This visit had been arranged as a respite for Mary's sisters who were the primary caregivers. Through a difficult summer Mary fought her impatience with her mother when simple tasks took forever. "I wrestled with my impatience, astonished and embarrassed that this woman, this mother, could elicit any emotion from me other than affection. I tapped my foot inside my head, all the while reminding myself that love is slow."[10] Unfortunately, the subject of death never came up.

> We could have talked about death as well, but now, watching her puzzled look about everyday trivia, I knew it would be too much for her. I wanted to tell her that everything would be okay. That my two sisters and I would be able to handle this transition in our lives. That dying is part of everything we are. That the God we both had confessed is no dream but a real Being who was orchestrating her last months and waiting eagerly for her arrival.[11]

But, like so many families, they didn't talk about "It."

## HOSPITAL RULES

There can also be humorous moments, too. It is difficult for some today to realize that hospitals once had strictly enforced "visiting hours." In most hospitals, precisely on the nose, a voice announced over the intercom that visiting hours were over. That made life difficult on families of dying mothers. There were other rules. For Liz Curtis Higgs's mom, a hospital room became home as she battled emphysema. Liz wanted some way to brighten those dreary winter days. So she would sneak in a Hershey's candy bar (her mother's favorite)—a significant infraction of hospital rules.

Liz asked nervously if the doctors would mind.

"They'll never see it!" Mrs. Curtis responded, opening the wrapper with all the enthusiasm of a child.[12] Liz watched her mother "eat" the evidence.

## At Christmas and Holidays

I wish there were a moratorium on dying during the holidays. Mothers do die on Christmas Eve and Christmas Day, but many cling to life through the holidays or until other special days are past.

Edith Kent's family made the decision to go ahead with the traditional Christmas buffet although their eighty-eight-year-old mother's health had been deteriorating and her mental state was unpredictable. Thirty-five family members gathered, each spending some time with Edith in her bedroom. After the meal, someone began singing a carol and others joined in.

> The songs must have reached her because she joined us. We called the rest of the family into her room. Mom sang all the words of each carol and hymn. Then just as easily as she had begun to sing, Mother stopped. That was her last Christmas.[13]

My mother had a way of letting me know that I was troubling her, "You're gonna be the death of me yet" and "Someday, you just won't have a mother!" Usually one was sufficient to alter misbehavior. Later, Mother dusted off the threats if I announced I was not coming home for Christmas: "Then you'll have to come for my funeral for it will just kill me if you are not here. It just won't seem like Christmas. . . ." And once she used an instantaneous guilt-evoking, "You know, this could be my *last* Christmas."

## Laugh or Cry or Both?

Barbara Bartocci yearned to talk to her mother openly about death. She had questions she wanted to ask, "Are you frightened? Do you wonder how we will remember you?" But those were not questions her mother wanted to hear, let alone answer. So, Barbara had to be content simply being with her, brushing her hair, patting and holding her hand. But one night the weight on her heart was too much. Barbara began to cry.

Crankily, Mom said, "For heaven's sake, Barbara, why are you blubbering?" I blurted, "because I'll miss you, Mom!" She looked past me, as if at something I couldn't see. "Well," she said. And then again, the single word, "Well." I took a breath. "Mom, is—is there anything special, a song or a hymn, that you would like played at—you know—at your funeral?" She said nothing for a moment. Then, grumpily, "No dirges. Play something with a little ooomph to it." We both laughed. We laughed! How peculiar and how wonderful it seemed that we could laugh![14]

## As a Favor to Me

Sons and daughters are overwhelmed by their powerlessness to alter the outcome. Many repeatedly ask a mother, "Is there anything I can do for you? Anything I can get you?" More than one adult child has moaned in a hospital corridor, "I feel so helpless!" or "I just wish there was something I could do." Sometimes there is.

Dave Anderson flew from Kansas City to Ohio to spend some time with his mother. He expected that being together as a family would delight her. So, when he asked, "Is there anything I can do for you," she asked Dave to change the goose's clothes! For years, Mrs. Anderson had a ceramic goose on the front porch of her home in Pennsylvania; each season she dressed the goose appropriately.

> So I found myself, a fifty-some-year-old son, taking what would be one of the last precious days I had to spend with my mother, driving hours to Pennsylvania to dutifully change the clothes on a ceramic goose. That's when it dawned on me. Mothers will always be mothers. You may be fifteen or fifty.[15]

One week after his drive to change the goose, Mrs. Anderson died. Dave reflected:

> My last gift to her was to change the clothes on a stupid, inanimate goose. Seemed like a small thing then. It's one of my most

precious memories now. Looking back, I'd have moved heaven and earth to give her joy during her last days with us. As it was, all I had to do was to dress a silly ceramic goose.[16]

Actor Kirk Douglas remembers his mother's last request. Hospitalized with multiple health problems, one Friday, at dusk, his mother stirred and asked what day it was. Hearing it was Friday, she reminded Kirk and his sisters to light the Sabbath candles. They had just started to light the four candles when nurses rushed into the room. With his mother in an oxygen tent, "We could have blown up the hospital," Douglas admitted. They left and lit the candles instead at one of Kirk's sister's homes, and he returned to report to his mother that the Jewish tradition had been honored.[17]

## LOVING DESPITE THE SILENCE

Anne Morrow Lindbergh, known for books like *Gift from the Sea* and *Bring Me a Unicorn,* lived the last ten years of her life in a cottage on her daughter Reeve's farm. Although Reeve dutifully looked in daily on her mother, in her last weeks of life, Mrs. Lindbergh chose not to talk to her. "To lose such an important listener in life," Reeve lamented, "is like losing my shadow."

> She neither talks to me nor acknowledges that I am talking. It's as if I am not there. I don't even exist. I take this much too seriously. I start thinking very fast, and the thinking is childish and irrational: she does not talk to me anymore because she no longer loves me. I know it isn't exactly true or is irrelevant—she doesn't need to love, she needs to be loved just now.[18]

Rarely can a child live with unanswerable questions. Consequently, some create "answers" that only compound grief. It is better, though harder, to continue to love despite the silence, recognizing the mother's need to be loved.

## When the Watching Is Tough

To watch a mother die is one of life's most demanding assignments. The watching, the witnessing, the helplessness to alter the script drains the soul. Rafael Jesus Gonzalez describes the experience he shared with his brothers:

> My mother lies in the hospital in a coma, tubes in her nostrils and veins, fed oxygen and fluids, buzzers and blinking lights monitoring her heart and lungs, her head shrunken, face wrinkled and dry, gray hair lusterless and matted on her forehead, her breathing harsh in her throat. A woman of remarkable strength, her body, even now, fends off Death, kind Death.[19]

The brothers sat awaiting the inevitable as have many siblings before and since. You may have been the sibling that announced, "No sense in all of us sitting here." Or you may have declared, "I'm staying. I am *not* leaving mother." Did you goad reluctant siblings into taking a turn of waiting? Sometimes the waiters wield words to shame a brother or sister who wants to bail out. How many promises are exchanged such as, "Will you call me if anything changes?"

Waiting.
I am sitting here waiting for the inevitable.
Everyone's gone home
    needed the rest, in case, God forbid,
    we find ourselves here another night.
Watching your mother die
    takes a lot out of you.
You'd rather be anywhere than here,
    yet I cannot stay away.
She was there when I entered this world.
I want to be here when she leaves the world
    and orphans me.

## PLAYING GOD WITH MOM'S LIFE

For some, there comes the inevitable moment when a doctor asks a son or daughter to "play God." The realization that we are entrusted with our mother's life can be sobering. Many do not find the decision making any easier when the doctor adds, "If it were my mother, I'd let her go." The decision can taunt long after a mother dies: "Did I [we] do the right thing?" Fortunate are those who hear a sibling say, "Yes, we did the right thing."

> I think that was the moment when I became an adult. The doctor handed me a paper and I signed. We had asked the doctor, our pastor, and we had prayed. The hospital stopped the antibiotics, intravenous fluids, everything except the morphine. To this day I believe we placed Momma into God's hands and he said, "Mavis, come home. They will be all right." —Bart

Second thoughts are troublesome when the decision-maker is the sole decider. Or when one is physically, emotionally, and spiritually exhausted. Even when physicians, friends, and pastors affirm, "You are doing the right thing," many children struggle with a nagging feeling that a decision was wrong or premature. I remember my sister, in tears, confronting me, "Are you sure we're doing the right thing?" Knowing that we could only prolong my mother's suffering, I responded, slowly emphasizing my words, "Look at Mom. That is not life! We are doing the right thing. We have to let her go." Mislabeling the practice of "pulling the plug" unfortunately only compounds the stress. One daughter expressed the feelings of many sons and daughters who have had to make tough decisions:

> You're never one hundred percent certain. There may be no right thing. Any choice can be wrong. You do the best you can do at the time. And you hope that someday your kids won't have to face these kinds of decisions.

## Hearing Mother's Last Words

Watching someone's mother die can be difficult for hospital personnel. Frederick Nenner, a social worker, described his interaction with two siblings. "The young woman speaks about how hard it has been to hear her mother's [last] words because she and her brother have not been ready to let their mother go."[20]

The decision is made to remove the respirator. The daughter leaves the room while her brother kneels by his mother's bed, "And this powerful man sobs." The tension is demanding for all who witness it. "We look with uncertainty, not knowing if we can bear this son's pain. The machine is disconnected, and, as we had thought, as we had said might happen, this mother breathes. Not as we would want her to breathe, but she breathes. When it is time, she will go."[21] The mother breathes through the night on her own.

> We return to the bedside the next day. We come one at a time. We are drawn to this mother whose heart keeps beating; we are drawn to this daughter and son who loved their mother enough to let her go when they wanted her to stay. . . . The children have brought in the pictures of a lifetime: a mother in her youth, a father long gone, the pictures that we all have in our homes, perhaps tucked away in places long forgotten. They bring in these pictures of a lifetime and begin the remembering.[22]

Most children cherish last conversations, whispered words, last smiles, last squeezes. My friend Becky Morsch, a physician, was there as her mother died.

> Mom very peacefully drew her last breath. . . . As the song says, I could practically "feel the brush of angels' wings" in her room those last few days as her angelic escorts stood by prior to their journey home. We rejoiced that Mom no longer suffered, and we grieved that she was gone from us. We still do.[23]

## BEING THERE AT THE LAST

> How I wanted to be there "for" my mother,
> in case she stirred and needed me.
> The best I could come up with was
> to be there "with" my mother
> in the incredible darkness of her dying.
> I relied on the assurances from nurses
>       that hearing is the last sense to go.
> Repeatedly, I whispered,
> "Mom, I know you can hear me. . . ."
> How I wanted her to respond,
>       just one more time,
> "Oh, Honey, you've come to visit me,
>       How long can you stay?"

The watching was easier with my sister present. We passed the hours recollecting the life we had lived with mother. Again and again one of us said, "Do you remember when Mom . . . ?" We sang through Mom's hymnal. Often in church, Mom had turned to me and said, "This is a good one." So we sang "the good ones."

Sensing my sister's exhaustion, I sent her home, announcing that I would stay the night. In the hours ahead, I became more tolerant of Jesus' sleeping disciples. At about 2 A.M. my body began protesting my resolve. One voice said, "Mom will never know. You can come back early in the morning." The other voice said, "*You* will know." I hastily scribbled a plea:

> God, I cannot chicken out and call it "a night."
> It's a tempting alternative to sitting here watching her die.
> I do not want my mother to die alone.
> She was always there for me, especially in those
>       middle-of-the night sicknesses
>       or when the bogeyman was menacing.
> Tonight is payback.
> Give me strength to last until morning.

Later that night I wrote:

I am sitting here wondering
when that final breath will come.
Is this the one? The next one?
How I condemn myself for complaining
    about the discomfort of this miserable chair.
But then maybe I am not supposed to be comfortable
    watching my mother die.

## WHEN THE DYING INTERRUPTS NORMALCY

For some, a mother's illness requires significant sacrifice—short-term and long-term. Given that adult children may be scattered across the state, country, even the globe, there is often a higher demand on those who live nearby. Anna Quindlen's first year away at college had provided delicious freedom from her mother's restrictions. When she was pulled back into her home world by her mother's illness, she divided time into two dimensions.

> "Before" for me was my freshman year of college, when I found myself able for the first time in my life to swear at meals and not be reprimanded, to go out at midnight and not have to tell anyone where I was going. "After" was the beginning of what would have been my sophomore year, when I found myself out of school, making meatloaf and administering morphine in a development house in the suburbs.[24]

A prolonged dying offers children opportunities to share their mother's last days with others.

They came. Grandchildren, neighbors, aunts, cousins, friends,
    with rehearsed good-byes,
        even though some knew she was in a coma.
    They came to offer words to her, to us.

The hardest was my Aunt Julia
    who death seemed to be picking on.
Fresh from her grief for her husband and her grandson,
    she came to say good-bye to her sister.
I asked her, "Do you still make meatloaf?"
My Aunt Julia's meatloaf was the best I ever ate—
    even better than my mom's.
How unfair that Aunt Julia had to grieve so many losses
    in such a short space of time.
Aunt Julia was just one of the courageous pre-mourners
    who came to offer a slice of comfort
    to three exhausted grown children,
    and two weary children-in-law.
"Call me," all of the visitors said,
    "if there is anything I can do. Anything."
And in that moment it did not sound like a cliché.

My mother's sister Ellen came and gave us some time to grab a bite to eat. Once Mom and Aunt Ellen had talked numerous times each day—just checking in. I invited my aunt to eat too, but she responded, "I will stay. This will give me a chance to be with Mary." My sister and I were not gone long. Who wanted to be off feeding your face when your mother died? When we came back, my aunt said, "We had a good talk." I must have been puzzled, because she added, "There were some things I wanted to say to Mary."

## To Go or Not to Go?

If "life happens while you are making other plans," then dying occurs while you are carrying out long-dreamed plans. Larry McMurtry, author of *Lonesome Dove* and *Terms of Endearment,* had long dreamed of a slow freighter trip through Polynesia. Given his mother's deteriorating condition, should he go or postpone the trip? His sisters were convinced that their mother would die while he was away. McMurtry weighed their apprehension. No one wants to be known as the son who was frolicking in Tahiti when his mother died in Archer City, Texas.

On the other hand, McMurtry noted, "I had been at my mother's side more or less daily for the past two years, watching her slowly fade." Her gradual deterioration had been difficult on him. "She faded as a photograph fades if it is left in too sunny a place, until only the dim outlines of personality remained. Her coherence would return now and then, but rarely for more than a few minutes."[25]

He made the decision to go, yet dutifully called from exotic ports of call. McMurtry, aware that more and more children in our mobile society have to make a decision whether to go or stay, pondered the dying process:

> Are we keeping her trapped in this twilight, with our visits and our mutterings? Is she responsive at all to the current of family interest, or is she merely rocking on, in a current of her own? Is there still a self there, a self that might realize that her first-born—myself—is nearly ten thousand miles away? Or has the self already retired from the dying organism? Is it easier to go with all of one's children gathered around, or does the fact that they're all gathered around only make it that much harder to go? Is our presence really a factor now?[26]

In roughly twenty-four hours, McMurtry traveled by air from Polynesia through Paris to Dallas, then drove to Wichita Falls, Texas. Walking into her room he discovered that his mother was still alive. Her eyes, he noted seemed unfocused; he speculated that perhaps in reality they "were focused on the Other Place, the abyss, the infinite, the one big adventure she was not long going to be able to avoid."[27]

"Hi, Mom, I'm back," McMurtry said, squeezing her hand but noticing no response. "I was there but she was far, as far as the Marquesas, near the place where the light leaves. She had, perhaps, been waiting, though, and perhaps knew I was home."[28] Hazel Ruth McMurtry died the next afternoon.

## A Mother's Vulnerability

Part of a son's or daughter's stress is witnessing the vulnerability of a mother in the last days. Many share Malcolm Boyd's experience: "It was hard to engage in a conversation because she was nearly deaf. So I resorted to a lot of nonverbal communication. I made a point of looking directly into her eyes, gesturing, smiling, and laughing." Malcolm even helped himself to bites of food off her plate, but toward the end his mother could not eat because of a blockage in her throat.

> Our visit always ended with saying the Lord's Prayer together. . . . After prayer I would sit quietly with her, holding her hands in mine. Often during the time she would close her eyes or else look out at the gardens. Before leaving, I embraced her for a few moments, holding her body close to mine. This essential physical communication bonded us close in spirit.[29]

Sometimes, a mother is too weak even to use the bathroom by herself. Mary Clare Griffin recalls:

> God, in my heart I knew we were coming to an end quickly, and I was terrified. She was so gallant, so dignified! I was weakened by it. I gasped back my tears. Don't you dare cry now, I willed myself. I very gently helped Mom sit on the toilet by supporting her from behind, letting her lean back against my body. . . . She tinkled and sighed, exhausted. "You're doing fine Mom, I got you" and together we rose. I patted her dry and pulled up her panties, still holding firmly to her waist.[30]

Many adult children cannot forget some of the tense moments in a dying that led to a reprieve, a stay of execution, or what Griffin calls "a sabbatical." Griffin, who lived in Idaho, had several long drives to Los Angeles hoping to get there in time. She could not afford to fly every time, although twice during her mother's illness, she sold a piano to buy tickets. Indeed, many sons and daughters fret anxiously that a brother or sister will not arrive in time. There are those adrenaline-pumping moments and then, as if the disease is only teasing, a reprieve. Many sons and daughters have arrived only to find their mother sitting up in bed, laughing.

How do sons and daughters get through the roller-coaster nights and days? Griffin's mother's friend Pasty comforted (and confronted) her: "Be strong for your mother. You're the only one who can give that to her right now, and she needs that from you. She loves you. Don't ever forget that."[31] Does that guidance sound familiar? Repeatedly, children are urged, "Be strong . . . for your mother" (or for your father who will have to live without your mother, or for other siblings). Some are told by observers well acquainted with the family dynamics, "You are the *only* one who can give that."

So, we buck up for another day's duty on the front line in a mother's dying. After one "code blue" experience, Mary Clare walked into her mother's ICU space: "Dwarfed by the machines and tubes attached to her small body sustaining her life, lying on the hospital bed, she looked less than real. Looked as if she went twelve rounds in the ring and got absolutely hammered. 'What were you thinking, coding like that? That costs extra!'"[32]

## MOMENTS OF DRAMA, LOUD AND SOFT

There are rather dramatic moments not unlike those in a made-for-TV movie. The dying also can be influenced by the nature of the mother-daughter, mother-son relationship. In some families, some things are best not talked about. Differences are never aired; yet, "some things" have ways of showing up in our minds as we wait and hope for any sign of change. Sometimes there are dreadful moments. Barbara Sherrod experienced one when her mother "exploded," chastising her for her practice of letting bygones be bygones instead of placing blame on others and holding grudges.

> After that visit, I cried as though I were a little girl whose heart had been broken, instead of a fifty-seven-year-old woman who had been through this sort of thing enough times to know better.

Of course, it fell to me to mend the fences with her. Like so many of that generation, Mother was incapable of apologizing.[33]

Barbara did what many daughters and sons have done. "I told myself that the episode merely signaled a marked decline in her physical condition, that it said little about how my mother actually felt about me." Easier said than done. "I'd heard the condemnation so many times before—though never so brutally—that I had a hard time convincing myself."[34]

A young jazz musician, on the other hand, organized his life around his mother, Daisy. In May 1935, when she was critically ill, her son was so stricken with what would now be called "anticipatory grief." Physicians were more concerned about *his* welfare. For three days and nights, he sat in an uncomfortable straight chair by her bed, often leaning his head onto her pillow. Duke Ellington said, "When my mother died the bottom dropped out."[35]

## ON MY WATCH

Despite the tension, Barbara Sherrod took her "watch" caring for her mother through the nights. "Here I am, spending day after day, hour after hour with her, holding her hands, smoothing her forehead, telling her she is loved. . . ."[36] "I pray in her ear, sing 'My Way' (her favorite song), and relate anecdotes of her children and her adored great-grandchildren." Repeatedly, she tells her mother that she and her sisters will be here as long as she needs them. Day in, day out, Barbara and her siblings' children sat waiting.

> I'd been dozing, waking, always listening for her sounds, watching her strain for another breath through her oxygen mask. Since early morning, I had noticed the waning of breath and movement. I'd wondered if this breath would be the last. But the last breath left when I wasn't looking. Quietly, peacefully, she slipped away, as though this were her own private business and nobody else's.

At first I felt I'd done wrong to be here at the last, that Mom would have wanted one of my sisters instead. Then I saw that she had honored me by dying on my watch. Before calling the nurse, I speak a prayer, then kiss her cold cheek for the last time.[37]

## BEING WITH MOM AT THE END

Barbara Bartocci was fortunate—she got to be with her mother for the last breath. She describes that All Saints' Day experience.

It grew quiet. I stood, stretched, then moved to her bedside. . . . Her face looked white and cold, so I brightened it gently with lipstick. I reached for her hand. It felt like tissue paper in mine. *Do you feel my touch?* I wondered. *Do you know, in your drug-induced coma, that I am with you?* It seemed to me that she was like a boat edging away from shore, drifting slowly, inevitably toward the horizon. Soon, I thought, the boat will disappear, and only the horizon, gray and empty, will remain. I spoke aloud, "Mom, your family loves you. And I love you." Her breath slowed, and then—had it stopped? I couldn't tell. I leaned forward. "Mom, have you left?" Her face was still. She looked peaceful. She had gone.[38]

Novelist Amy Tan had a different waiting experience. She and three sisters and brothers moved into their mother's room in a care facility, sometimes sleeping on the floor, for the last three weeks of her life. At times as many as twenty people were in the room.

She hung on, hung on, even after the doctors said she was going to die any minute. And we realized, she's not going to leave her own party! She's having too good of a time! So we quieted down, and when we did, she died after that. I'll never forget her last breath. She was unconscious and on morphine, but her last breath was like a little cry: "Ahhhhh!"[39]

Asked to elaborate, Amy Tan continues:

She sounded like a surprised child. Like one who was delighted
by something. It was very interesting, and quite amazing. It was
a very holy moment, similar to when people witness a birth.
Much sadder, of course, but I find such tremendous peace and
strength in that moment.[40]

Tan concluded that such moments offer a "great opportunity"
for both mother and daughter.[41]

## IF ONLY I HAD BEEN THERE

I was not there when my mother died. I had been at her side for
several days. When a nurse convinced me that Mom could "go on
like this for days, perhaps another week," I protested that was
impossible. "Oh, no," the nurse responded. "I've seen it many
times. Your mother won't die before her time." I thought of the
phrase often used in my family when someone would not do something "until she was good and ready."

I pondered the nurse's assessment as I stood staring out the
window into the winter darkness. What should I do? If there was
little I could do for Mom, I could fly home, lead my grief group,
take care of some business matters, and come back. I prayed that
God show me what to do.

Finally, I sensed a release to leave. I kissed my mother good-
bye and whispered in her ear that she had fought a good fight and
it was all right if she wanted to go before I returned. At the door, I
paused for one last mental snapshot.

Exhausted, I flew home to Kansas City. It was late when I
arrived home. Holding my breath, I retrieved phone messages. No
calls. Good! Mother was still alive. In that moment, rather than
unpacking, I stumbled into bed and mumbled, "God, be with us
all, especially Momma."

I had just fallen asleep when the phone rang. Without bother-
ing to turn on lights I walked into the study and picked up the

phone. I knew that Mom had died. The accusations began. I had not been there for my Mom's last breath. I had failed my mother!

In the saddest voice I have ever heard him use, my brother-in-law Charlie said, "Your mama's gone." I asked to speak to my sister.

"We don't have a mother anymore," Norma wept. I asked for details. My mother had not been alone. My brother and sister and their spouses had been called by the nursing home, "You'd better come." We agreed to talk the next morning and after I hung up the phone, I exploded with rage.

"God! I *knew* this was going to happen! How could you let this happen? I was not there when Mom died. I *could have* been there! Didn't I ask you to show me what to do? I am so mad at you! I could have been there!" I ranted like a madman until exhausted. "God, I am so angry at you. But right now I need a good night's sleep. Help me sleep."

I slept soundly. I had not set an alarm and could tell it was late because of the light at the edge of the bedroom shades. Got to jog. Reality hit me as soon as my feet hit the floor: Mom died! No, it was just a dream. I had dreamed this before. As I sat on the edge of the bed, awareness slapped my heart. My sister and brother had both confirmed it. Mother . . . is . . . gone. My family prefers the words *gone* and *lost*. People do not die. They are "gone."

> We rely on kinder synonyms in such moments
> as if a word can defuse the sting:
> gone, passed, expired. . . .
> Anything but the blunt "died!"
> Whatever, when your mother dies
> an exclamation mark is in order.

As I jogged, I mentally listed everything that needed to be done, calls to be made, items to pack. I began notifying friends. Soon the "I just heard . . ." calls and E-mails began coming in.

I was now a motherless child.
Mary Catherine Eckert Smith's motherless child.
I aged that morning.
I felt older, alone, abandoned.
Never have I felt so alone.
I had wanted to be there for her and I wasn't.
Never mind that I had been at her bedside
until 4 A.M. three mornings before.
Never mind that my brother and sister had been with her.
I was not there!

My absence would draw comment. Southern folk naturally inquire, "Were *all* the children there when she passed?"

I can remember many times when Mother had stood in the airport and waved good-bye to me. Why wasn't I there for her ultimate departure? I live with that mystery. In the months ahead I talked about my anger at not "being there." After one presentation, a lady approached me.

"Have you considered the possibility that your mother did not want you there when she died? Maybe she was waiting for you to leave."

I found some comfort in that possibility, particularly after reading accounts and listening to people talk about their mother's "holding on." I suspect my anger has more to do with my own fear of dying alone, my hand unheld, my death unwitnessed.

## A LITTLE GIRL BY THE WINDOW

Some young children are not allowed to participate in the dying. In fact, a family may collude to keep a mother's prognosis from a child. In 1892, Anna Roosevelt contracted diphtheria after a surgery. Exhausted from years trying to cope with her alcoholic husband, Anna did not want to live; the children were divided up "for the time being" among family members. That winter day before Christmas, as eight-year-old Eleanor stood by a window pondering the confusion in her life, an aunt, Susie Parish, walked in and told her, "Your mother is dead." That death took away the child's hope of winning her mother's love. Eleanor would live with a menagerie of ifs: "If she had been more jolly, more attractive, more compatible, better behaved, would her mother have lived?"[42] These questions haunted her throughout her life.

> With her mother's death, she became an outsider, always expecting betrayal and abandonment. . . . For the rest of her life her actions were in part an answer to her mother. If she were really good, then perhaps nobody else would leave her, and people would see the love in her heart.[43]

Eleanor Roosevelt became one of the greatest women achievers in the world. One has to wonder how the deaths of her mother, brother, and father—within eighteen months—nudged her toward incredible public service.

In this chapter, we examined the experience anticipating a mother's death; in the next chapter, we look at unanticipated deaths.

## A PRAYER

> Give me strength sufficient for the demands of this day.
> Give me the courage not to anticipate tomorrow
> in order to avoid today.
> Give me grace not to turn my head away from the
> bloody awe-full business of losing
> such a source of strength. Amen

# 2. THE PASSING

*The death of a beloved flattens and dulls everything.*
  —Maya Angelou[1]

*Mother's death had been the most determining, the most profound, the most influential event of my life. It had become my organizer, the focal point of my identity and the standard to which I compared and contrasted all other stresses of my life. An F on a paper couldn't rankle me much when I remembered what I'd faced at seventeen.*
  —Hope Edelman[2]

*As a bereaved adult, I grasped for some reason, cause, or explanation for this accident. There was an overwhelming sense of wanting to "make some sense" out of this accident that had destroyed my belief in an orderly universe and control of "my world."*
  —Jeanine Bozeman[3]

*But at any age, the loss of a mother is a special bereavement. To be cut off from the one who bore us, nourished us and taught us the first and deepest lessons of life, leaves us lonely in a way no other deprivation can.*
  —F. J. Bowman to Harry S. Truman[4]

YOUR MOTHER WILL DIE. HOW, WHEN, and under what circumstances is the unknown. Unfortunately, there is no shortage of traumatic ways for a mother to die: murder, catastrophe, terrorist acts, automobile and industrial accidents, suicide. I was moved reading the experience of a nine-year-old boy in Goma, Congo, following the eruption of Mount Nyiragongo. He and his mother ran from the lava. As some point, he looked back and his mother wasn't behind him. The boy was found wandering barefoot near the soccer stadium that was being used as a temporary shelter. He is one of many children who lost mothers that day. How does he grieve for her?

What will become of those children whose mothers died in the terrorist attacks on September 11, 2001, especially those too young to fully comprehend the loss? How will the toddlers, the babies ever know how precious, wonderful, heroic their mothers were?

Who has it easier: those who know their mothers are dying or those whose mothers die suddenly, without warning? In this chapter we examine the experiences of those who had no warning. One woman tells this story:

> We were driving to the mall to pick out a dress for her granddaughter's wedding. "My first grandchild is getting married!" she fussed. "That makes me an old lady." "Well, how do you think it makes me feel?" I asked. Before Mother could answer, we were broad-sided. I woke up in intensive care asking for her. . . . When I saw my daughter's face, I knew. Mom had died instantly at the intersection, near the entrance to her favorite mall.

The death was only the beginning for Sara. The wedding had to be postponed, she had a long recovery with a broken pelvis, and she had to endure "the second trauma"—the long court battles. The driver of the car that struck them was intoxicated; this was his third accident. Twice, people had been injured. Sara laments that she could not attend her mother's funeral or even contribute to the planning.

## WHY?

Jeanine Bozeman seldom left her father's side during the hospitalization for the last two months of his life. The night before he died, he said to her, "I want you to care for Mother. I know it won't be easy, but all I'm asking is that you do the best you can." Without hesitation, Jeanine agreed. Over the next eighteen years, the daughter worked at keeping the promise.

Bozeman had driven her mother back to her home in Alabama and was returning to New Orleans to teach her graduate classes. In a few days Bozeman and her husband would drive to her mother's for Thanksgiving.

As Bozeman reached her home, her mother was in an automobile accident in Alabama. The driver of the car, Bozeman's sister-in-law, had failed to stop at a stop sign. Upon notification, that promise taunted Jeanine. "I had failed to take care of her."

> Why had I taken mother home? Why couldn't I have waited until Thanksgiving Eve? Was it so that I and my husband could enjoy a break from the care giving? Was I selfish and irresponsible? Why didn't I stay with her and "prevent" her from getting into my sister-in-law's car? The "what-ifs" all came flooding in and overwhelmed me.[5]

As the Bozemans drove to Pensacola, where her mother had been transferred for brain surgery, Jeanine prayed that her mother would live until they could get to the hospital. "Somehow I must have felt that my presence could save her."[6]

> For the next nine weeks my life was a nightmare endured in the hospital waiting room, anxiously awaiting the precious fifteen minutes with Mother. . . . The ups and downs brought hope and denial, sorrow and despair, anger and impatience—an emotional roller coaster. During those days living out of a suitcase, sleeping on the floor of the waiting room, and jumping when the telephone rang, I experienced disorganization and total lack of control. I vacillated among those feelings and experienced

volatile emotions, especially toward the driver of the car, as I saw Mother suffer a heart attack, pneumonia, heart failure, surgery, convulsions, and finally death.[7]

As a social worker, Bozeman had helped many people walk the shadowed valley. She was now a daughter desperately wanting her mother to live. Her mother died.

## ARRIVING TOO LATE

Weather has a way of interfering with the best-made plans of daughters and sons planning to visit their mothers. A huge snowstorm had shut down New York City. Two days passed before Dorothy could take the subway to her mother's nursing home. As she trudged the last blocks in the thick snow, she anticipated her mother's joyful question as she arrived for every visit, "But, darling, how did you find me?" Dorothy always answered, "I'll always find you, Mama."

Stamping snow off her boots, she proceeded to the reception desk and signed the register. The receptionist did a double take. "Who are you here to see?" This question struck Dorothy as odd because the receptionist knew her from her previous visits. "Didn't anyone call you?"

"No. What about?" Dorothy's mind raced ahead to answer her own question. "What? Tell me, tell me. What! Tell me!"

The receptionist summoned a doctor for an embarrassed explanation. Her mother had died early that morning.

They let me see her. She was in her room. It was very cold. The window had been opened wide to stanch the smell of death. Her mouth was open. Someone had closed her eyes. They had wrapped her in a large green plastic bag. They had attached a tag to her toe. They shouldn't have done that.[8]

A simple bureaucratic mix-up. It happens. "Yes," as one grieving daughter shared of a similar circumstance, "but not to my mother!"

## LAST ACTS

Some dying mothers are still mothers. Minnie Taylor, pregnant at age fifty, had fallen down a circular staircase in her home. Now as she lay in a rural Texas hospital, someone brought her daughter Claudia, who had just turned six, to see her.

"She looked over at me," Claudia recalled, "and said, 'My poor little girl, her face is dirty.'" Minnie asked for a wet washcloth. Slowly and carefully she scrubbed her daughter's face. She fell back onto the bed and burst into tears.

Minnie Taylor died soon after her child left. At least Claudia, who grew up to become Lady Bird Johnson, first lady of the United States, knew that her mother had died. Mr. Taylor chose not to tell his sons, Antonio and Tommy, away at boarding school, for almost a year. Antonio held that against his father for the rest of his life.[9] How could a father not tell a child that his mother had died?

Anne Morrow Lindbergh died on February 7, 2001, just as her daughter, Reeve, and son-in-law, Jon, were entering the door of her cottage. Reeve, like many children, protested her mother's timing.

> I've been told that people sometimes do that. Maybe it's hard to die with your children in the room, so that you try to slip away when they are near but not exactly with you. Maybe they pull at the heart-strings too much, make you doubt the wisdom and distract you from the work of your departure. You start to worry about how your dying will affect them, and whether they will be all right after-ward. Oh, dear. Should I? Shouldn't I? Are they really ready? Is there anything I have forgotten to tell them before I go? Do they all have their mittens and their lunch money? But she went without us.[10]

## WAITING

As a controller,
the waiting is driving me nuts!
I've divided everything into categories:
    Things I can do something about

Things I can do nothing about.
Sometimes, it takes a moment to weigh a situation
    but the longer the "cannot control" list,
    the briefer the "can control" list
and the less I have to do but sit and witness
    my mother's dying.

## THIS CAN'T BE HAPPENING!

The timing of life events can be outrageous. February 1884 was an emotional roller coaster for a young New York assemblyman. The assembly was seriously considering five of his bills, which was significant for someone in his first term. The Republican establishment nudged one another, "Keep an eye on him. He's going places!" After his wife had given birth to a baby girl on February 12, Theodore passed out cigars and accepted congratulations until the telegrams arrived: Come home *now!*

Five hours later, as he walked into his home, his brother moaned, "There is a curse on this house." He bounded up the stairs and into his bedroom and found Alice, his wife, dying. As he held her, he pleaded, "Let her live!"

Late in the night, he slipped from the room and walked down a flight of stairs into his mother's bedroom. Theodore held "Mittie," his mother, until she died at 3 A.M.

He returned upstairs and held Alice until she died that afternoon. The thick grief in the house was punctuated by the cries of a two-day-old child. Theodore slashed a large *X* across the day's page in his diary and scribbled, "The light has gone out in my life."[11]

Days later, he followed identical rosewood caskets out the Fifth Avenue Presbyterian Church. In a daze, he had to be led like a child from the graves. Friends lamented that his promising political career was shattered. How could any man survive such a blow?

Seventeen years later, following the assassination of William McKinley, forty-two-year-old Theodore Roosevelt became president of the United States. But he never forgot Valentine's Day, 1884, when his mother and wife died.

## WITNESSES TO ACCIDENTAL DEATHS

Accidents happen, even to mothers, and sometimes their children are among the witnesses. The impressions left from such a scene can be indelible.

I once thought princesses had lives of ease. Well, princesses have mothers, too. What was grief like for Princess Stephanie of Monaco? Stephanie was seventeen—a typical teenager—when she and her mother drove off a cliff in Monte Carlo after a fierce argument. Stephanie's trauma was sensationalized by the supermarket tabloids. Years after the accident, Princess Stephanie still hears whispered accusations. "My mom died and everyone said I was responsible. You're already in the grief of losing a loved one, and suddenly everyone points at you. And it's like they're saying, 'Why is she still around?' . . . You try to convince yourself you don't care what people say, but it hurts."[12]

Had you said to twenty-one-year-old Dwight Samples, "You're going to kill your mother" that December night in 2001, he would have laughed. He was just a guy with a souped-up car seizing a "show off" moment that went terribly wrong when a car pulled onto the highway in front of him. Given his speed, there was no time to avoid plowing into the car driven by his mother, Diane Samples. Reportedly, at the scene of the accident when told who he had hit, he insisted that she receive medical care first.[13]

The day began innocently with fourteen-year-old Fergus Bordewich and his mother, LaVerne Madigan, riding horses. On a familiar trail, his mom nudged her horse into a faster pace. Minutes later, she screamed that she couldn't stop Pepper. "I will save my mother," Fergus thought.

> I know what to do. I've seen it done in a hundred Western movies. I will gallop next to my mother, lean from my horse, seize her bridle, and pull Pepper to a halt. I kick General forward, "I'm catching up," I cry. But this is fantasy, because I am not catching up at all, because the faster I gallop the faster Pepper goes, steadily widening the gap between us, not saving my mother but panicking her horse.[14]

Trying to dismount, his mother fell from the horse. By the time Fergus reached her, blood was flowing from her forehead and mouth. Her head had cracked open either from hitting the road or the horse had kicked her. She did not respond to Fergus's pleas. Fergus ran some distance to a house and pounded frantically on the door. A woman stared through the screen, listened, then slammed the door in his face.

Other riders who came upon the distraught boy and his mother assured Fergus that his mother would be all right and that he should return the horses to the stables. He believed them.

Fergus's father met him at the barn. They drove to the hospital and sat outside the emergency room. Finally, as a doctor approached, Fergus's father asked, "How soon will she be able to leave?"

"Your wife is dead," the doctor replied.

A boy's desire to ride horses with his mother turned into a nightmare. As they drove back to the lodge where they were vacationing, Fergus convinced himself that his mother would be waiting for them. She wasn't. In that confronted reality, Fergus's father broke down and cried—the first and only time that his son had seen him cry. "I felt ashamed for him and went outside into the ripe air. The sky had cleared, and it had become a splendid day. . . . I could hear motorboats on the lake and the shouts of water-skiers. I listened to my father and thought, I am not going to cry. And I didn't."[15]

Over the next years, again and again, Fergus would replay the events of that morning. Why had he insisted that they ride? Twenty-eight years after the accident, he recalled his mother's fall. "That moment would never stop reverberating, radiating its meaning outward through my life and everything I touched. It would become an eternal moment, ever occurring, . . . unhindered by the laws of time and space. . . . It was always terrifying. I would never stop hoping that it would turn out differently."[16]

## YOUR ETERNAL MOMENT

Every mother's death, by accident, illness, or natural causes, becomes "an eternal moment, ever occurring." The recollection of your mother's death, or where you were when you learned of your mother's death, seems to play endlessly, also "unhindered by the laws of time and space." Do you agree with Fergus's assessment that his mother's death became the benchmark that "marked the end of my childhood and the beginning of all that came after"?[17]

Anna Quindlen knows about the benchmark impact of a mother's death: "I learned to live many years ago. Something really bad happened to me, something that changed my life. . . ."[18]

## HOW MUCH PAIN CAN WE TAKE?

How much pain can a son or daughter take? Life seemingly wants to find out. Jamie, eighteen, and John Law, nineteen, returned home from a high-school trip to Disney World to discover that their father had died the previous night. Five days later at the committal service their mother collapsed. John raced her to the hospital, but still she died. Life caved in on two adolescents. Soon their mobile home was repossessed, and the insurance company refused to pay any benefits because Jamie and John were underage. After John decided to take his sister with him to the State University of West Georgia where he planned to enroll in a few months, a roommate disappeared with their apartment deposit. John reflects on his string of losses: "It's like I'm in the middle of a big storm or something. So many things have kept happening. And just when you think it's about to die down, something else happens."[19]

## UNTIL THE LORD TAKES ME

Molly Kughn loved the one-hundred-year-old farmhouse outside Abell, Oklahoma, in which she had lived for fifty-three of her seventy-six years, the last twenty alone after her husband's death. Her son Gary had tried to persuade her to move into town but she wanted to stay on the farm. One afternoon, alarmed by television reports of a massive storm, he phoned her, "Get into the cellar!" The phone went dead. Fearing the worst, he jumped into his car and raced fifty miles. After using a chainsaw to cut trees that blocked the road to his childhood home, he found his mother's body.

"I'm sad because my mother is gone. But the medical examiner told me she didn't suffer much pain, and I'm grateful for that." A number of mothers died that spring day in 1999. It is not always how a mother dies but how a son or daughter interprets the death. "Her greatest fear was that she would have to leave the farm, to move into town. She would say, 'I am not going to leave here until the good Lord takes me.' A grieving son concluded, 'And he did.'"[20]

Gary added words voiced by many readers, "I miss my mom."

## A PRAYER

My mother has died.
No matter how many euphemisms I create
    to make to defang the passing,
the reality sounds brutal in my heart.
I cannot alter the suffering she endured at the end.
Save someone's mother today from dying the way
    my mother died.
Be with me in these days of "trying on" mourning.
Bring into my life those who understand the language of this landscape.

# 3. THE MOURNING

*People must be given the opportunity to hurt out loud.*
　—Lady Bird Johnson[1]

*The fraternity of the bereaved is perhaps the oldest fellowship of humankind. Within the fellowship cluster those who wear the badge of particular loss—who speak a language never chosen and learned in pain and tears. One such cluster of the fellowship is those who become orphans—children without parents—regardless of chronological age. On January 20, my sisters and I became members of that fellowship— mid-life orphans, receiving the mantle of full adulthood, bearing the title of the older generation of our family.*
　—Kay Collier-Slone[2]

*My mother and I shared so many things: lollipops, lace hankies, hair barrettes, girlish secrets, and a passion for chocolate-covered cherries. We sang camp songs and she taught me how to make s'mores. She showed me how to make a great meatloaf and even lump-free gravy. In fact, my mom taught me everything—except how to live without her. I was forty-three when she died, and I was devastated.*
　—Darcie Sims[3]

THE WORDS *grieving* AND *mourning* ARE sometimes used interchangeably, but Alan Wolfelt clarified a subtle distinction. Grieving "is the constellation of internal thoughts and feelings that we have" when a mother dies. Mourning, on the other hand, is "the outward expression of our grief."[4] Grief is what we feel; mourning is what we express.

Jesus' promise, "Blessed are those who mourn, for they will be comforted" (Matt. 5:4), sounds outdated in this culture. Blessed? The reality is that many suffering motherloss go uncomforted or are minimally comforted; some mask their feelings to avoid the criticism that they are "still mourning." Some mourners fail to allow others "in" to bless their experience. Some consider "didn't shed a tear" to be a badge of honor.

## WHAT'S THE BIG HURRY?

We mourn for mothers in a mourning-challenged society that pressures individuals to "get over it." Lynn Davidman experienced anguish standing in a Jerusalem cemetery as her father was buried next to her mother:

> That night . . . I was transformed into a thirteen-year-old girl whose mother had died. "I want my mom," I repeatedly sobbed, mourning the lost opportunity to have known my mother over the course of my life, to have her know me now as a woman. And I have wondered about the many ways in which my life would have been different—and easier in significant respects—if my mother had not died when my brothers and I were young.[5]

Until that moment, Lynn thought she had handled her loss well. Many sons or daughters deflect questions convincingly, "I am doing fine. Thank you for asking." Soon, friends stop asking, "How are you doing?" and begin complimenting, "You are doing so well. I don't know how you do it." Or they belittle their own grief skills, saying, "I don't know what I will do when my mother dies." If we do not make a serious attempt to mourn now, mourning is forced underground and will lay dormant, awaiting an opportunity to be reactivated by a significant life event or transition in the daughter's or son's life.

## MOURNING THE MOTHER YOU KNOW

Leo Rosten asserted, "There is no such thing as a bad mother."[6] Some readers might angrily disagree, saying, "You never met my mother!" Quincy Jones had a testy relationship with his mother, Sarah Jones. Lloyd, his brother, was her caretaker until he became critically ill with cancer; Sarah died six months after Lloyd. Jones reflects on his loss of brother and mother in so short a period:

> All he ever wanted was for her to nurture and validate him, to feel proud of him. That's all he ever wanted. That's all any child wants. It's something he never got. There's no feeling like that desire to hear your mother say—just once—"Well done, son, I love you." That feeling never leaves you, even when you're grown. He would have given anything in the world to hear that.[7]

Mothers are not perfect, and some are far from perfect. Mothers can be ne'er-do-wells or villains—cold, cruel, vindictive, pitting one child against another. "Joan Crawford had nothing on my mother," one nurse mused. An old southern expression echoes in many adult hearts: "If Momma ain't happy, ain't nobody happy." Some children, whether young or adult, must cautiously interact with mothers to avoid saying the wrong thing. Even mothers can have a dark side.

Some incriminate themselves for their lack of visible mourning following a mother's death. The late Katherine Graham, former publisher of the *Washington Post*, acknowledged, "It seems almost inhuman to cry at superficial books and movies or when upset or angry, but not when I am deeply shaken, as I certainly was not only at my mother's death, but at [my husband's death]. . . . " Looking back, she assessed, "I couldn't believe she was gone. She had led a long and extraordinary life and left her distinctive mark in many areas—certainly on her children and grandchildren, and even on the two oldest great-grandchildren."[8]

On the other hand, Graham conceded, "My mother was no longer there . . . to resent, to emulate, to rebel against." Her mother had aged poorly. "Too many years of too much food and drink, combined with too little exercise, had made her overweight as well as arthritic." After she lost weight, she did not gain a great deal of mobility, but she recovered: "She was back again, exercising her authority, criticizing, and arguing."[9]

Sometimes adult children struggle with the woman who became a better grandmother than a mother. Some envy the relationship their children have with her. Others wonder how she could have changed so much.

As Helen died, she wanted a high-drama bedside reconciliation worthy of a made-for-TV movie. Unfortunately, her four daughters wanted reconciliation but only if their mother would "own" her physical and verbal abuse. Repeatedly, the mother had snipped that her daughters would never amount to anything. Through the loving nurture of an "adopted mom," the sisters blossomed as human beings and competent professionals. All they wanted was an apology. It was hardest on Cora. She is a therapist who has heard her own story in many of her clients' narratives.

> I finally came to the conclusion that she just wasn't capable of the truth. It would have been too painful. After we achieved, she milked the "after all I've sacrificed for you" routine. She could not admit that she had nothing to do with our achievements. We achieved in spite of her and proved her prophesies wrong.

The words "I'm sorry" could have made her daughters' mourning easier.

Mourning can be an invitation to some sons or daughters to revisit their wounds, to wander through their memories, reexamining, and reinterpreting them. Given the dysfunction rampant in many families, accurate remembering feels like betrayal. In our hearts, we hear, "How dare you remember me like that!"

Some mothers are not capable of giving children what they emotionally and spiritually need. Yet some adult children cling to the fantasy that someday she will. Thus the son or daughter must mourn the collapsed fantasy as well as the death. Young Eleanor Roosevelt could hardly mourn a mother who considered her ugly and told her, "You have no looks, so see to it that you have manners."[10] Linda Richman could hardly mourn a mother who, on her death bed, humiliated her: "Linda, you got fat!"[11] Some mothers wound but leave no scars or bruises. One woman told me, "I know I am *supposed* to mourn my mother, but . . . I'm not." There is, however, no statute of limitations on mourning a mother's death.

Arthur Ashe withdrew from life emotionally after his mother died. After witnessing his father's anguished mourning, the six-year-old boy did not dare ask questions that might upset his father. Tennis provided an escape. Ashe wrote:

> I don't remember grieving over my mother. She died, and life moved on. My father told people how my response to the news, as he sat crying his eyes out between my brother Johnnie and me, was simply enough. "Don't cry, Daddy," I consoled him. "As long as we have each other, we'll be all right." I don't remember any of that.[12]

Not surprisingly, Ashe developed a reputation for being aloof. Some colleagues conjectured that the aloofness was influenced by the deaths of his mother and grandfather within a twelve-month period, two significant losses for a six-year-old.

> I have understood that this quality of emotional distance in me . . . may very well have something to do with the early loss of my mother. I have never thought of myself as having been cheated by her death, but I am terribly, insistently, aware of an emptiness in my soul that only she could have filled.[13]

## Shielded from Mourning

A half century earlier, another six-year-old was overwhelmed by a father's mourning. Claudia Taylor had not been allowed to attend her mother Minnie's funeral. Days later when the minister called on her father, he commented that Minnie Taylor was "better off in heaven than on earth." Her father pointed at Claudia and angrily demanded, "Who's going to take care of that little girl?"[14]

Witnessing her father's rage, Claudia "made up her mind not to be the burden he feared. I just felt so sorry for him. . . . I had no feelings at all for myself."[15] Indeed, many can be so busy monitoring the mourning of others in the family—or taking care of them—that they ignore their own.

During cotton-picking season, Taylor stayed at his general store twenty-four hours a day (or chose to stay as a defense against his grief). He made a pallet for Claudia on the floor near the caskets he sold.

> One night after he put her to bed, [Claudia] asked her father, "What are those long boxes?" Taylor looked at the coffins, hesitated a moment and then answered, "Dry goods, Honey, just dry goods." It's difficult to imagine that Taylor would have been so insensitive to his daughter's feelings. . . . As a matter of survival, she learned early on to keep her emotions buried, symbolically locked in a coffin in her soul.[16]

A few months later, Taylor sent Claudia by train to Minnie's family in Alabama. "He dressed her in a nice dress, tied a bonnet around her head, and put a sign around her neck, 'Deliver this child to John Will Pattillo,'" her great-uncle. Today such insensitivity would constitute child abuse, but this six-year-old perceived the trip as an adventure. "I knew the conductors and porters would take care of me."[17] Unfortunately, the Pattillo elders in Alabama warned Claudia's cousins not to talk about Minnie's death. The child mourned in familial silence.

## HIDDEN MOURNING

Douglas Gresham, at age fourteen, was away at boarding school when his mother, Joy, died. During the trip home, he said, "I kept my mind filled with everything I could think of to hold back the flood tide of my grief."[18]

Dropped off at the porch of his home, Douglas opened the door and made his way to the common room where he found his stepfather standing by the fireplace. "Oh, Jack," Douglas cried out. His stepfather quickly crossed the room to embrace him. That was "the only occasion upon which any physical demonstration of our love for each other ever occurred."

"Jack, what are we going to do?" Douglas asked.

"Just carry on somehow, I suppose, Doug." Advice given early in Douglas's mourning influenced the terrain of his loss. Finding Douglas in the garden his mother had loved, Fred Paxton, the family gardener, wrapped "his huge arm gently around Douglas' shoulder, and whispered, 'Don't cry son.'" Doug reminisced, "He had no more words, and so we stood together in mute and mutual sorrow."[19] Hours later, Jean Wakeman, a family friend, told Doug that "She expected me to comport myself like a soldier on parade, God bless her! I did not weep at the ceremony . . . I stood at attention and held my head high."[20] Douglas reflected further, "I was horrified at the very idea of breaking down and showing my grief in public, so I shut it up within me, hidden away deep in the darkness of my mind."[21]

Many of us have witnessed hidden mourning. Millions watched Princess Diana's sons, William and Harry, follow her casket in the funeral procession demonstrating the "stiff upper lip." It's not only young men who are urged to keep tight reins on mourning. These days, females are also told to be strong. Olympic gold medalist Jackie Joyner-Kersee writes:

> I didn't cry until a year later. The coaches had been concerned, because I hadn't cried or anything. I was always seen as being happy, happy, happy. Finally, I remember, the other girls on the team were talking about what they were going to get their

mothers for Christmas. It was strange. It just hit. I was trying so hard to hold it all in, and it all came out.[22]

Blessed is the son or daughter who is permitted, encouraged to mourn.

## THE NEW MOMMY

Some daughters become the "new" mommy in a family structure, particularly if the father is grieving in isolation, undependable, or is pursing a new romantic interest. Some children volunteer to step into the void, while others are appointed. Someone has to make sure that "life goes on" for the children. Family roles must be reshuffled so that life can have "some semblance of normalcy." So, the child/mother mothballs his or her mourning to deal with the practical realities. Hope Edelman writes: "Like most families that lose a mother, mine coped as best it could, which meant, essentially, that we avoided all discussion of the loss and pretended to pick up exactly where we had left off."[23]

You do not delay mourning for a mother by avoiding it or by throwing yourself into your work; rather, you delay reconciliation with the loss.

## BEING STRONG

Many families have siblings who are "strong" and siblings who "take it hard" or "go to pieces." Sometimes, there can be a surprise flip-flop from previous family dramas. A brother or sister may mourn unpredictably. Some individuals assume mourning is something to be disposed of as quickly and efficiently as possible—a grief pattern that I label "lite" grief.

Some well-intentioned individuals, including ministers and counselors, misquote scripture to discourage mourning. Paul's wisdom in 1 Thessalonians 4:13, for example, reads: "But we do not want you to be uninformed, brothers and sisters, about those who have died, so that you may not grieve as others do who have no hope." Yet the verse is often offered as "comfort" in truncated form: "We do not want you to mourn." Individuals who never met our mothers sometimes counsel, "Your mother would not want you to . . . ," and we have a right to demand, "How do they know what my mother would want?"

Sometimes siblings, spouses, or our own children also try to halt the grieving process. "Now Mother [Grandma] would not want us carrying on like this . . . . " Soon after notification of a mother's death, we begin to hear the "shoulds" about how to mourn. "You should look on the bright side," I was told repeatedly, "Your mother is in a better place." But it is hard, at that moment, to think about that "better place." Hearing such advice, Phyllis threatened, "If one more person from mother's church tells me, 'Your mother's in a better place,' I am going to scream! I don't want her in 'a better place' walking on streets of gold and singing with angels. I want her *here*. When I walk in that house I want it to smell like my momma has been cooking something good!"

My colleague, Doug Manning, offers wise guidance:

> Don't let anyone take your grief away from you. You deserve it, and you must have it. If you had a broken leg, no one would criticize you for using crutches until it healed. If you had major surgery, no one would pressure you to run in a marathon the next week. Grief is a major wound. It does not heal overnight. You must have the time and the crutches until you heal.[24]

## MOURNING IN THE WORKPLACE

In some work settings, an adult child is allowed five days off after the death of his or her mother, but then is expected to return "over it." "I owe, I owe—it's off to work I go" is a legendary explanation of why people work. It also explains why some motherloss mourners return to work immediately. But would you want a surgeon operating on you who had buried his mother the day before? Blessed is the person who does not have to immediately return to work after the death of a mother. Many mourners, however, have no options: no work, no income.

Some believe that going back to work will do a mourner good. It fits so well with the counsel, "Stay busy." Unfortunately, today's workplace is rarely conducive to mourning. Some have been surprised that the colleagues who sent cards and beautiful flowers are uncomfortable with ongoing mourning. One supervisor chided a friend of mine, "When my mother died, I only took a day off." Mourning for a mother can be difficult to explain to a supervisor or colleague who has never been touched by motherloss or who has a strained relationship with a mother.

## MISSING FACTS

Some children do not get full details of the death. When Rosie O'Donnell's mother died, her father was blunt: "Your mother passed away."[25]

"I didn't even know what that meant. And that was the end of the discussion." How could this child mourn without some explanation? Moreover, the father decided that the children should not attend the funeral mass. In a matter of hours all evidence of her mother disappeared from the home. "There was nothing left."[26] So, this mourning child created a fantasy that her mother had become tired of the responsibilities of five children and had run off for a new life in California but "one day would certainly return."[27] After a neighbor told the child that her mother had died with hepatitis, "figuring we were little and didn't know what it meant," Rosie found a dictionary. "I was in the fifth grade, and it said a disease you get through dirty needles. I remember thinking, in a 10-year-old's rationalization and justification, that it was from sewing."[28]

Unfortunately, like Claudia Taylor and Arthur Ashe, Rosie O'Donnell and her siblings lost their father, at least in spirit. "He seemed perpetually 'away' in his own little world, unable or willing to exert a healing guidance to his devastated family."[29] As a result, this child mothballed her mourning and became the homemaker, caring for her siblings and for an ailing grandmother.

## MOTHER'S STUFF

Malcolm Boyd writes: "Here before my eyes and at my fingertips, was the residue of someone's entire life, the record of a human existence."[30] A mother's death forces a son or daughter to deal with her possessions. Whether furniture, art work, or even fabric that she was going to use "some day," collectibles, clothes, the good china—a decision must be made about all of it. How and when possessions are dispersed fuels family feuds worthy of the Hatfields and McCoys. Oh, no one is physically wounded—but the sense of family diminishes.

> The work of discarding and saving,
> boxing and bagging,
> trashing and storing
> can be heart-taxing work.

Boyd describes the fatigue while sorting through his mother's possessions:

> As I tried to sort through my mother's things, at times I laid my body on a couch, or sat down in a chair, mustering strength to complete an arduous task. I opened all of Beatrice's drawers and closets. I examined the contents of shelves, nooks, and crannies. Her dresser drawers were filled with underwear, stockings, and nightgowns. In closets were dresses, suits, coats, hats, and shoes. In the kitchen were dishes, silverware, pots and pans, canned goods, and a great iron kettle that had belonged to my grandmother.[31]

For Boyd, an only child, the exploration prompted questioning. "Each object seemed to tell its own story, or was somehow a part of her story. I had to pick and choose."[32] For some, the cleaning out, keeping, throwing away is too final. Who wants to dump their mother's "things" into garbage bags?

In some families, one daughter or son often will rush this part of grief, getting things over and done with, while another sibling resists, hoping to deal with this aspect of grief later. In the process, old sibling conflicts can resurface. Given the mobility and hectic schedules of individuals, some insist that immediately following rituals may be the best time—or only time—to do this necessary work. Siblings may seek to bolster their point by demanding, "Why wait?"

By end of life, some mothers have few possessions, which might make this task easier. In some cases, the move to assisted living or into a nursing home required a two-step dispersion: initial and final. Dick Gilbert writes of the pain he and his siblings experienced when they had to close his mother's house:

> I remember having to close down an eleven-room house, with fifty-three years of memories, in two days. It was so unfair. The pressures of the calendar robbed us of remembering dinnerware and furnishings, pictures and height measurements by the kitchen door, outdoor parties and sneaking a kiss with that first boyfriend or girlfriend.[33]

The distribution of a mother's possessions often prompts troubling existential questions, particularly for middle-aged children. "What will become of my most treasured and intimate objects?"[34] Who will appreciate what I have valued?

For my friend Kay Collier-Slone and her sisters, their mourning intensified when a large moving van backed into the driveway: "Surely the biggest red, green, and, yellow moving van on the road. . . . The treasures of this home were going to be delivered to our scattered family" in eleven residences in three states.[35]

Kay did well until she watched the cherry dining-room table carried out the door. "You okay?" one mover asked. Kay smiled and replied, "Lots of happy memories around that table." This was not just any old dining-room table—although that was how it was listed on the manifest—it was a symbol of family history.

> We realized later that while long-dreading the moment when we would close the front door for the last time, we had not thought

about the departure of the van. Suddenly it was Saturday evening. The rooms were empty of all but the remembered; the van doors were shut. We moved naturally into the family ritual of departure, walking the team to the van.

Two beeps on the horn had long been part of family good-byes in the Collier family. "Today, we realized, the ritual could not really be completed. The corner would be silent. No one to sound the two-beep salute."[36] The three sisters were surprised, then, when the driver tooted the horn twice as he reached the intersection. Days later, upon delivery in Atlanta, the driver was puzzled when told of the family's good-bye ritual. "I don't know why I blew that horn. I've never done it before."[37]

At the last stop, as "we talked about new traditions for old treasures," Morris, one of the movers, disclosed that his mother had died earlier that year. Now, as an only child, he faced the first holidays without his mother. Kay, a compassionate caregiver, offered solace to another mourner. Again, as the van pulled away, Kay heard that familiar sound: the two honks from the moving van.

## SETTLING MOM'S ESTATE

You never know what kind of family you are in until you settle an estate. Nothing can sabotage mourning like a brawl over an estate. I knew that theoretically. I learned it experientially after my mother died. I am amused when people say confidently, "Oh, we would *never* fight over mother's stuff. Not our family." Not all family feuds are launched over stocks, real estate, bonds, artwork, collectibles, silver, or crystal. "Junk" ignites many emotional free-for-alls.

If a mother dies before a father, the estate is not settled, but her possessions must be distributed or given away. Fathers may see mourning as a task to be completed: "Best get at it" as Laura discovered when she called her father several days after her mother's funeral.

"Just wanted to see how you are doing today, Dad."

"Oh, I've been keeping myself busy—doing little things that need to be done."

"Like what?"

"Oh," he answered, "just getting rid of some of your mother's things." Laura felt uneasy.

"What things, Dad?"

"Well, I've pretty well gone through her clothes and the china and the crystal. I won't be needing that stuff. So I just got rid of it."

"Dad, what do you mean, 'just got rid of it?'"

"Oh, I boxed it all up and took it down to Goodwill."

"Oh, my God!" Laura screamed, hanging up on her dad. "Oh, God, no!" she moaned as she grabbed her car keys and dashed out the door with one agenda: to get to Goodwill before . . . En route, she dialed her sister's number and screamed: "Meet me at Goodwill. Now! Dad's gone nuts and given Mom's stuff to Goodwill."

"What stuff?"

"I'm not completely sure, but I heard him say 'china and crystal.'"

"I'll be there in ten minutes." Both sisters prayed frantically that their mother's good "stuff" would still be there. On their way, both of them revisited memories of the elegant way their mother would set the table for special occasions and holidays. The china had been in the family for decades. How could their father just give it away without consulting them?

Fortunately for Laura and her sister, the "stuff" was still in boxes in the back of the store. The staff had been too busy to go through it. The sisters explained their dilemma to the manager and he allowed them to take the boxes their father had left. To this day, both remain stung by what almost happened. What if it had been a slow day and the stuff had already been priced and shelved? Or sold? Or what if they lived in another city or state?

## TAKING APART THE SYMBOLS

Barbara Bartocci, after reading a disturbing article on family feuds over estates, wrote her brothers, "Promise me we'll never fight over our parents' stuff." Then came the day for Barbara and her brothers to close their mother's house permanently. One brother showed up with packages of sticky red, blue, and yellow labels to mark choices. Okay, but who gets to select first? When one brother suggested the time-honored process of rock, paper, scissors, the siblings burst into laugher. "Somehow," Barbara remembered, "starting off with a child's game made things easier."[38] Some sons or daughters already have full houses, apartments, trailers, or whatever.

Some spouses question them, "What are you going to do with this?" Some siblings become serious sentimentalists—no jelly-jar drinking glass goes unnoticed or unvalued. Bartocci remembered the day:

> As we chose, we reminisced about our selections: the Chinese cookie-jar Rob remembered from his childhood; the silver coffee urn that had special meaning for me. We were taking apart the symbols of our parents' life together, yet I felt a poignant awareness of the intangibles we had received—the love, laughter and solid values.[39]

Unfortunately, not all families find the dividing pleasant. Selections become a petri dish in which resentments grow for years afterward. The grabbing and snatching—let alone a grown sibling screaming the equivalent of "Mine!"—might be forgiven, but not forgotten, especially when rehearsed to anyone who will listen.

## UNPREDICTABLE SIBLINGS

Stuff disappears even in friendly families. Gail remembers:

> A quilt of my mom's just disappeared. For years whenever I asked, "Wonder what happened to that quilt?" my sister never

responded. One night my niece and her husband were in town to attend a convention and came for dinner. I have several quilts hanging on the walls of my home. In the course of an evening's conversation, the subject turned to quilts and I described my mother's guilt. "Oh," my niece said, "that sounds just like the one in my mom's bedroom." My sister had taken that quilt! No wonder she had evaded my questions. I should be happy that it is still "in the family," shouldn't I?

## ONE BOX

Neighbors seeing me carrying the box
would have assumed I had purchased a new computer.
The recycled Gateway box—
with its characteristic black on white patches—
was packed with the emotion-laden relics of eight decades
of my mother's life and five decades of my life with her.
When I shipped it, the postal clerk asked,
"How much is it worth?"
"Millions" I wanted to answer,
but any antique store dealer would have snapped,
"I don't think so!"

The box stayed unopened and inside the front door of my home for months. As I came and went I reminded myself that I should unpack it. But to take out the objects would add a note of finality that I wanted to evade—they belonged in my mother's house.

The treasures included her first baby picture and the Christmas wreath I had bought her that last Christmas in what became a futile attempt to inject some holiday spirit into her dying process. How my mother had loved Christmas! In a few months, that wreath hung on my front door as I mourned a first holiday without her.

## LYNNE'S LAMENT

Lynne had promised herself to leave the cell phone at home for the funeral and burial. In that community, there was a tradition of family members standing around talking in the cemetery after a committal, but Lynne noticed that her sister, brother-in-law, and their grown children left after the minister's final "Amen." Lynne lost track of time but was chagrined when her cell phone rang! "I thought I had left this at home," she apologized.

"Answer it," a friend responded. "It might be important."

"Lynne, I hate to bother you," said a neighbor of her mother's, "but there is a moving truck in your mother's driveway. And people are carrying stuff out of the house. . . ."

"Call the police!" she shrieked. "Someone's broken into Momma's house!" Family members sprinted for cars and frantically drove to her mother's house. Arriving, they discovered her sister, brother-in-law, and their children helping themselves to her mother's possessions.

"Mother's not even in the ground and you are grabbing stuff!" Lynne sobbed. "Have you lost your mind? What have you taken?"

"Only taking what's rightfully mine!" With that she turned and left the house, slamming the door. A quick walk through made clear to Lynne what had been taken.

"I don't believe this!" Lynne sobbed. "I don't believe my sister would do this! Not on the day Momma was buried!"

In some families, possession is the proverbial nine-tenths of the law. Lynne could not bring herself to use legal remedies to challenge the injustice. Needless to say, her mourning for her mother has been greatly complicated by the estrangement from her sister, particularly because some of the items were ones that her mother had wanted Lynne's children to have.

"I lost my mother and my sister the same day." Lynne and her sister have not spoken since.

## EXECUTORS

Too many mothers die without wills or with outdated wills that do not reflect current relational and financial realities. Some family members plead, "Can we all just get along?" Old unfinished quarrels may lead siblings to take sides. "You wanna put it to a vote?" only complicates the mourning process. "I was outvoted every time," laments Cindy. "Every time."

Some siblings cannot mourn because they are serving as executors of a mother's estate. "I didn't have time to mourn for mother," said Art. "I had ten million details to manage. Fortunately, my siblings were supportive. But the attorney told me some outrageous stories of siblings coming to blows or suing each other."

Some mourners have been stunned by disclosures in a will. John laughs, "I had always been told we would split everything four ways. Equally. I knew I was in trouble when the executor said to me, 'I have some good news and some bad news.' The version of my mother's will that I had read was not the will that was probated. My brother got far more than his one-quarter. He got some of mine, too!"

## A DEFINING MOMENT

For most children there comes a defining moment when they begin to integrate the loss into their lives. Father James Johnson wrote his friend Harry Truman after the death of Martha Truman: "All alone I lost my mother and tho I'm a priest waiting on the dying and preaching thousands of funeral sermons, I've learned the real reality of death comes only when your mother dies and then it seemed the bottom of our earth drops out. Yet we can't keep them forever. God knows best. . . ."[40]

Sometimes, simple things can set off a new outburst of mourning.

> Anger, I'd always thought, had to be object directed, and though
> I focused some of mine toward my father, I didn't know where
> to direct the rest. Without a distinct target, it shot out at wholly

unpredictable moments: on the telephone with the electric company, over dinner with my boyfriend, at the history paper I couldn't concentrate on long enough to write.[41]

The scolding that "Your mother wouldn't want you to carry on like this" has been around a long time. Lottie Healy Jackson wrote President Truman in 1947, "I am sure she would want you to look bravely into the future and to be courageous."[42] Indeed, a mourning president, despite the polls and pundits, courageously ran for reelection and pulled out a stunning victory. The famous picture of a grinning Truman holding up a newspaper with the mistaken headline announcing "Dewey Defeats Truman" would have made Martha Truman proud.

Bill Clinton once described the first time, after his mother's death, that he had an "I've got to tell Mother about . . ." experience: "I recall the first time I really realized she was gone. I used to call her every Sunday night. . . . So I came in on Sunday night from my trip [to Europe] and I was into the kitchen and all but had the phone picked up before I realized: 'My God, I can't do that.'"[43]

## A PRAYER

Blessed are those who mourn
    for they shall be comforted.
Lord, I have heard this beatitude
    since Mother taught it to me.
Now, in her absence,
    help me to discover its truth.

# 4. THE BURYING

*Undertaker, undertaker, please drive slowly . . . for that passenger that you're carrying is my mother for to carry her away.*
   —Southern traditional folk tune

*We are never prepared—even if we think we are.*
   —Barbara Bartocci[1]

*We buried my mother in as much of a celebration of life as one can, because she was so full of life.*
   —Ronny B. Lancaster[2]

*And yet this is a bad business at any age. It is a pure squealing about our own mortality. It's a stern reminder that some day my own daughters are going to be orphans.*
   —Bill Tammeus[3]

*I feel a very great sense of deprivation.*
   —Winston Churchill[4]

EVEN IF YOU HAVE PONDERED THE POSSIBILITY of your mother's death—someday—few are prepared for the decisions and details that drive reality home. Some children inherit a nightmare of traditions, choices, and options. Mercedes Bern-Klug, a social worker, estimates that about seventy decisions must be addressed, including when to bury, where to bury, and what type of services to hold.[5] Simple decisions can become excruciatingly complicated and can distract from grief. Fortunate are those whose mothers have a "pre-need" funeral policy that spell out details and represents their wishes. Some mothers always plan ahead.

Kemble Anders, defensive end for the Kansas City Chiefs, took four-and-a-half days away from training camp to bury his mother. He said, "I was busy with all of the [funeral] arrangements, the insurance, all that stuff. This was my first time doing something like that. I didn't know there was that much red tape to it."[6] The "red tape" complicates mourning for many sons or daughters.

*Going home*
This is not like other trips.
It's a once-in-a-lifetime trip:
    I am going home to bury my mother.
I knew it would happen some day—
    just didn't know
    it would be this day.
I had plans
    but my "to get done" list dissolved
    with three words:
    "Your mamma's gone."
Actually, it was my mother that had gone "home."

## MAKING ARRANGEMENTS

The making of arrangements after a death can take on many qualities. It can be painful or challenging or humorous. Some grievers wedge the rituals into busy schedules. It is not uncommon to read in an obituary, "services pending" or "services to be held at a later date." Jack Nicklaus was playing in the PGA Championship in Louisville when his mother died. Mrs. Nicklaus had long been afraid that she would die during a major tournament. Having previously made her last wishes known to her son, the veteran golfer played his round knowing that she would be pleased. "It will be a big day for both of us," he explained. "I'll have her in my thoughts. Maybe it will inspire me to play a little better."[7] Making arrangements could wait for her son's work to be done.

Nancy Keller's mother, Dorothy, died the day before Thanksgiving. (Nancy now tells friends, "Don't die on a holiday. Everything just becomes more difficult.") Nancy made the arrangements:

> We went into this room with many caskets. I was amazed at the wide variety of choice. . . . I just wanted a simple designed casket made out of a beautiful wood. There ahead of me was a gorgeous casket with a sign "Marquis" written on it for the model name. That was my Mom's maiden name and also [my deceased brother's] middle name. I thought: that's it. That is my sign from above. I told the funeral director that was my choice and commented on the beautiful wood.[8]

When the funeral director mentioned that the wood was oak, the decision unraveled. "All of a sudden," said Nancy, "my head kept hearing what my mother had repeatedly told me. 'I grew up with oak [furniture] during the depression. Everyone had oak. I couldn't wait to get rid of the oak and get cherry.'" Nancy resumed looking and finally chose a pecan wood casket. Fourteen months later, she reflects, "I think she would have been happy with my choice for her."[9]

Frank McCourt depicted the courageous spunk of Angela, his mother, in his memoir *Angela's Ashes*. In his second volume of memoirs, *'Tis*, he described the planning for Angela's funeral. When the three McCourt brothers—Malachy, Alphie, and Frank—met for breakfast before the meeting to arrange the funeral, Frank was stunned by how much Alphie ate. "How can you eat so much with your mother dead?" "I have to sustain my grief, don't I?"

At the mortuary, the funeral director placed a large album on the desk in front of the brothers and turned to the picture of an elegant casket priced at slightly less than ten thousand dollars. "Very nice indeed," noted the director. The McCourts kept turning pages. When the only casket left was still beyond their budget, Malachy spoke up, "What is the absolute rock-bottom price?"[10] Before the director could answer, Frank reported that one week earlier, their mother had informed him that she wanted to be buried in Ireland.

"Mom," Frank had challenged her, "do you know the cost of transporting someone your size?"

"Well," she said, "reduce me." Her sons laughed heartily.

The funeral director was not amused. He offered the "rock bottom" price for embalming, viewing, and cremation. Malachy questioned why they had to pay for a casket that was going to be burned. "It's the law." "Then," says Malachy, "why can't we just put her in a Hefty trash bag and leave her outside for collection." The brothers laughed and the mortician left the room.[11] The McCourt irreverence, while it might offend some, is a valid way of coping with the stress of making the arrangements.

Malcolm Boyd, who as a priest has worked with many sons and daughters in planning a mother's services, observed that one of life's great challenges is "to try and see inherent humor, absurdity, or irony in any situation," including a mother's death.[12]

## A TRIO OF RITUALS

Three rituals are commonly scheduled: the visitation (also called the viewing, wake, calling hours), the funeral (memorial service if there is no body present), and the committal. Today, many families want alternatives. So, there may be a funeral *and* a memorial service; there may be additional services in cities or communities where the mother had lived. There is a growing trend for private "family only" services, particularly committals.

## THE VIEWING

Viewing a mother in a casket can be a collision with reality. Kweisi Mfume recalled, "The thought of seeing her in a casket, eyes closed eternally, was too much for me to bear."[13] Frank McCourt reminisced, "No one can say my mother looks peaceful in her coffin. All the misery of her life is in the face bloated from hospital drugs and there are stray tufts of hair that escaped her plastic razor" and the embalmer's attention.[14]

For some, the contrast between the memory of their mother in life and this viewing can be dramatic, particularly if the death was a suicide, homicide, the consequence of an automobile accident or severe trauma. Siblings may exchange impressions: "She looks like she's asleep" or "She looks so peaceful" or "She looks twenty years younger."

My mother had attended lots of viewings. In our phone conversations, she often talked about another friend's death. Frequently she commented, "She made such a beautiful corpse." Mom never commented on the casket or shroud. How I hoped that during the visitation someone would say, "Your mom made such a beautiful corpse." No one did.

Arthur Ashe contrasted two memories. One, the last time he saw his mother alive. Dressed in a blue corduroy dressing gown she stood in the doorway watching him eat breakfast. "And then," he wrote, "I remember the last time I saw her, in a coffin at home. She was wearing her best dress, made of pink satin. In her right hand was a single red rose. Roses were her favorite flower."[15]

## SEEING THE CORPSE

We siblings and spouses gathered in the lobby of Ratterman's Funeral Home for "the walk" down to the parlor. My sister began crying when the director beckoned us to follow. Then I started crying. This would be the first time I had seen my mother dead. My sister and brother had spent time with her at the nursing home before the funeral director came. They knew she was dead. Now I would "see" for myself. "Seeing is believing," my mother always said.

We looked into the casket and gasped: "This isn't Mom! We're in the wrong parlor!" We spun on our heels to confront the funeral director.

"Oh, yes," he replied, "that is your mother."

"That *cannot* be our mother! It doesn't look a thing like her."

"That is your mother," he repeated.

We turned back to the corpse and leaned in for a closer examination. "This cannot be her!" my sister insisted firmly.

I decided to take charge. "You all stay here," I said in the hushed tone of voice. "Mr. Trailor, could I see you, in private?" He escorted me to his office.

"Okay," I began, "I am a graduate of Mid-America School of Mortuary Science, so level with me. What is the problem with the embalming?"

Mr. Trailor explained the difficulties he had encountered "preparing" my mother's corpse. He apologized, "We did the best we could. Your mother had so deteriorated . . ." I walked back to the parlor.

In such circumstances, however, a picture can be worth a thousand words. Because I had feared that my mother's corpse would not be everything we wanted, soon after arriving in Louisville, I went to a nearby copy shop with several snapshots taken before I was born. "I need something for my mom's visitation."

"My mom died last year," the young employee said. "Let me see what I can do. Come back in an hour."

I walked around downtown Louisville. In the days before malls and shopping centers, our big adventure had been to ride the bus downtown and spend the day shopping on Fourth Street. Every year, on my birthday, my mother took me to a photographer's studio, which was then located across the street from where the copy shop now is. As I walked, memories danced. There was one department store that we only "looked in" because we couldn't afford anything sold there. My mom said that store was "for the rich people who lived in the East End, but it won't hurt nothing to look."

"Someday, I'll have enough money," I had boasted confidently, "to walk in here and buy whatever I want."

Today seemed a good time to honor that promise. I walked into that store and bought a pair of shoes. I walked back to Kinko's and was stunned with the young man's creativity. He had enlarged the pictures and had mounted them on easels. At the visitation, those pictures, not the corpse, became the center point of conversations. One pictured my mother in a dress, riding a tricycle, and laughing. (My mother was seldom captured well in photographs. Generally, she took the pictures; never do I remember a photo of her laughing.) Another captured my mother and dad standing in front of a comfort station—laughing. I hoped someone at the visitation could tell me what had been so funny. Verda Taylor, my mom's friend for a good half-century, smiled, "You know, that is exactly how your mother looked the day I met her."

We could have saved money on the casket. No one noticed. Those attending the wake noticed pictures "made special" by a young man at the copy shop who knew what motherloss felt like. It was the first of many kindnesses shown to me by veteran pilgrims on the motherloss trail.

Some memories were about me. More than one conversation began, "I remember you as a little boy . . ." Many included the words, "Your mother was so proud of you . . . she would always tell me about you, or where you had been in the world. Mary was so proud of all your books. . . ."

It was not a sad wake but a joyous celebration of one remarkable woman named Mary. My mother frequently said, "Now don't go to any trouble on my part"; however, people went to a lot of trouble to come stand a while in a parlor at Ratterman's to make three siblings feel better.

Although some sons and daughters thoroughly dislike the idea of "viewing" the corpse, many find the experience helpful. Winston Churchill wrote a friend about viewing his mother, Jennie Randolph Churchill:

I wish you could have seen her as she lay at rest—after all the sunshine & storm of life was over. Very beautiful & splendid she looked. Since the morning with its pangs, thirty years have fallen from her brow. She recalled to me the countenance I had admired as a child when she was in her heyday.[16]

Baseball great Jackie Robinson had not arrived in Los Angeles in time to see his mother, Mallie, alive: "I felt I couldn't go into the room where she lay. Somehow I managed to and I shall always be glad that I did. There was a look, an expression on her face, that calmed me. It didn't do anything about her hurt, but it made me realize that she had died at peace with herself."[17]

## RECEIVING THE VISITORS
Visitations provide a way for the children to interact with those who come to pay respects.

There's something about a visitation that does a heart good!
Hugs from those who normally do not hug.
Tight hugs from generally "lite" huggers.
Stories of graces received, burdens shared
    kind "let me know if there is anything I can do's"
    and the promised assurances of "better days."
Those moments remembered years later,
    send me to visitations
    for friends whose moms have died.
I received, so now I give.

Art Linkletter made a name for himself with the phrase, "Kids say the darndest things." Well, condolence bearers can say the darndest things, too. One experienced mourner advised, "You have to overlook them—they don't know any better." Some callers sling old, tired, worn out platitudes.
"She's in a better place."
"She's out of her suffering."
"You wouldn't want her back; she was suffering so much."
In the grief groups I lead, we laugh as participants recall the

faux pas that evoke groans and moans of, "I cannot believe they actually said that to you!"

A visitor might even arrive with an agenda. My sister, brother-in-law, and I had slipped out for dinner with my friend Dale, who had driven two hundred miles for the visitation. (My sister could not believe a friend would go so far out of his way.) As we walked back into the parlor, my brother approached me, "There's someone who wants to talk to you," pointing to a woman standing at mother's casket. I walked over and said, "I am Harold Ivan, Mary's youngest . . ."

"I know who you are! You put all that filthy sex in your books!" I was incredulous with this attack on my book *Singles Ask*. Who was this woman?

"Please," I interrupted, "*not* in front of my mother." (My mother was not timid when someone criticized her son, "the author.") I stepped back from the casket and the woman followed, never missing a beat: "Filth! Sex. Sex! Sex!" Was this someone's idea of a joke? I saw someone I wanted to talk to and excused myself. What made this woman think my mother's visitation would be the appropriate venue to express her disapproval of my writing?

Despite this unique and disturbing occurrence, my mother's visitation made me a believer in wakes. Considering mother's age and the depletion of her social network over the years, I was surprised by the large turnout of old friends, neighbors, extended family members, and parishioners from mother's church who came bearing condolences and wonderful stories.

Some come bearing eloquent eulogies to a life lived.
Even the strugglers who fumble over words,
offer the gift of presence. A simple sentence like,
"I thought a lot of your mother" is packed with meaning.
Sometimes elegant phrases
come from individuals you wouldn't expect to compose
such welcomed wordgifts.

## THE FUNERAL

Few children forget the day of their mother's funeral. One grieving daughter remembers: "The day of her funeral was beautiful. Colorado in November—and, strangely enough, the air still warm, the grass still green, and many fall leaves still bright on the trees. Clouds like beaten egg whites scudded across the sky; geese wandered among the gravestones at the cemetery."[18] If God was annoyed with my anger, I was hoping God wouldn't hold that against us when it came to the weather that day. The funeral home and cemetery are not far from the Ohio River; bitter winds had been known to blow through that neighborhood in February. I woke up and peaked through the curtains, elated to see bright sunshine. No rain, no ice, no snow, no wind. I couldn't think of anything worse than a funeral procession in cold rain or howling winds.

Not everyone attends a mother's funeral. In some cases, someone decides that a daughter or son is too young. One father told me, "My son wouldn't know how to act." (I wanted to answer, "Who does?") But age is not the only factor. Eleanor Roosevelt, Lady Bird Johnson, and Barbara Bush did not attend their mothers' funerals; Ernest Hemingway was too angry at his mother to attend, but he paid for the funeral anyway.

Barbara Bush, then living in California, was pregnant when her mother died in Connecticut, and her father did not want her to make the long trip home. She remembered "what a lonely, miserable time that was." Fortunately, she had recently been back home for a family wedding. "My sister, Martha, and her great husband, Walter, took charge of all funeral plans. And I sat in California." George Bush took the day off and invited friends from Yale living in the Los Angeles area to spend part of the day with his grieving wife. Mrs. Bush remembers that those friends "were marvelous to me."[19]

## THE EULOGY

One element in a funeral or memorial service—some would insist the *key* element—is the eulogy. Many daughters and sons spend incredible time trying to find the right words to capture a mother's life. For some, simple is more memorable. Others would like to do a eulogy but cannot imagine getting through it. Liza Minnelli's words for her mother, Judy Garland, were read by actor James Mason: "It was her love of life which carried her through everything. The middle of the road was never for her. It bored her. She wanted the pinnacle of excitement. If she was happy, she wasn't just happy. She was ecstatic. And when she was sad she was sadder than anyone."[20]

Sometimes a son or daughter's words become a template for others who must someday write a eulogy for their mother. Patti LaBelle sang the eulogy at her mother's funeral. She wrote:

> The words flowed from my mouth, but I knew they were coming from someplace else. Someplace my mother had been the first to see in me. . . . I sang as I've never sung before. . . . I was thirty-four years old, and for the first time I saw one of life's great truths with crystal clarity: A girl never really becomes a woman until she loses her mother.[21]

One morning I was called to a beauty salon by a friend. "I need you to help me write a eulogy for my mother." Because I am a writer, friends believe that, whatever the occasion, I have a way with words.

"But I didn't know your mother."

"No, but you're good with words." As he shampooed and clipped patrons' hair, I asked questions and wrote down answers. Patrons offered suggestions. During a couple of hours in a busy salon, a eulogy took shape.

A delayed memorial service allows more time to hone the eulogy. Sometimes, eulogies are something of a committee project, with siblings offering, rejecting, or vetoing words and phrases. Some keep the eulogy a surprise. Others choose a sibling, spouse, or grandchild to hear the rough draft. Some stand and preface their remarks with a qualifier, "I'm not good at making speeches" or "I just hope I can get through this," and then eloquently eulogize a mother's life and influence.

How do you sum up eighty-three years in a few minutes?
Gotta keep this on a tight schedule—
    other families need this space
    to honor their loved ones.
I want people to know something about this woman
    I have called Mother, Mama, Mom.
Some knew her as Mary.
Some knew her as Miss Mary.
Some knew her as Mrs. Smith.
So how do I sum up eighty-three years
    in a few minutes?
I can't—but I will, at least, begin.

## CONDUCTING THE FUNERAL

People questioned me, "How could you conduct your mother's services?" Given the insensitivity of her pastor in not visiting her ("Your mother is old and has Alzheimer's. What could I possible say to her?"), I had no choice. Doing the services was a way of thanking my mother for all the sacrifices she had made. I relied on a string of frequently breathed "God help me's. . . ." And God did. I suspected that Mom had approached the Great Throne earlier that morning and said, "My son will need a lot of help today." I think mothers still lobby in heaven.

The crowded parlor had more the feel of a reunion than a funeral. I was nervous; twice, I introduced the same friends to my brother. As my watch ticked toward the ten o'clock service, the funeral director asked if I would like a few minutes alone and led me to a small room. What I intended to say was written on five note cards—note cards like the ones on which my mother had written her recipes—although she had seldom needed them. I would need these cards today. I was not about to "wing" my mother's funeral. Rarely have I felt so alone as I did waiting for the large hand to hit the twelve. As the soft organ music began, Mr. Trailor cracked the door and said, "It's time."

Those two words echoed like thunder on a spring night. *"It's time!"* How could it be time to do something so final? I was determined we would not start late. That would not do for Mary Smith.

I walked into the chapel and took my place behind a podium, standing in the same spot where I had conducted my father's funeral eleven years earlier. I wish the service had been recorded because it is a blur in my mind, although I have leafed through the note cards trying to prod my memory. I do remember that people were gracious afterward, expressing words such as "Your mother would have been so proud of you."

You only get one chance to do your mother's funeral. There are no retakes or "once more from the top." I got through it, as my sister noted, without breaking down. That night I lay awake wondering if I had done my best for this woman, who had repeatedly given me her best.

## MAKING SPECIAL

I dislike generic, "straight-from-the-manual" funerals. I wanted, in the words of the University of Washington anthropologist, Ellen Dissanayake, to "make special" for my mother.[22] Because my mother's favorite gospel song was "And When the Battle's Over We Shall Wear a Crown," a gold crown rested on top the pink-rose casket spray. As I concluded the homily, I called attention to the crown.

"All her life, my mother sang that song—confident in her faith that in some distant moment, she would wear a crown." Stepping to the casket, I lifted the crown and then turned to her corpse.

"Mom, this isn't much of a crown—it's just a symbol—but I am confident that you are wearing your crown today." Then I placed the crown over her folded hands.

When I asked the director to remove the floral spray from the casket, people began to nervously shift where they were sitting.

What was going on? The spray always stayed on the casket. Then, with a cloth, I polished the lower lid of the casket. I turned to face the mourners.

"You know my mother was quite a handshaker—she should have been a politician. So, as you come by the casket to leave, place your hand on the casket and leave your fingerprints so Momma will know you were here." Heads turned and eyes asked, "Did I hear correctly?"

As the organist played, they walked by my mother's open casket. I stood at the foot of the casket and watched some lightly touch the casket as if it were too hot to touch. Ralph Ferren, my mother's Sunday school teacher for a number of years, paused, tears streaming down his face, and placed both hands on the casket. My Aunt Ellen lovingly stroked the casket, "I'll see you soon, Mary."

The director closed the casket; the bearers took their places. As the organist began "Onward Christian Soldiers," we processed down the hall to the hearse. Mom was going for her last ride.

Sitting in the hearse and waiting for the procession to begin, I began to breathe easier. The funeral was over. I had gotten through it. Suddenly, the hearse began moving. I watched the familiar sights of the neighborhood through the passenger window.

"You know," the driver began, "I've seen lots of things in my years as a funeral director, but I've never thought to ask people to leave their fingerprints on the casket. Would you mind if I suggest that to families?"

"I would be honored if you would." As a diversion from my thoughts, we talked about changes in funeral traditions. I stiffened as we approached Bacon's Shopping Center. How many hours had Mom and I spent there shopping or visiting with my sister who worked there? On my visits home Mom would say, "Let's drop by and see your sister." Shoppers getting into or out of their cars paused to take in the slow-moving procession. We drove through the gates of the cemetery and along the winding lanes. As we approached the mausoleum I moaned, "God, help me!"

One last time I looked at the tribe—to the children, grandchildren, and great-grandchildren, men and women—who had carried Mom out of Ratterman's and now had carried her into the mausoleum chapel. My brother had questioned having female pallbearers. "This is almost the twenty-first century," I prodded him, "we need to get with it" ("get with it"—another of Mom's favorite expressions). I think he was moved watching his daughters bear their grandmother. I turned to these people Mom had so loved. "I want you to place both hands on Mom's casket." The bearers did.

I read words from *The Book of Common Prayer,* which millions of sons and daughters have heard. Then we said our good-byes and hugged those not staying for the church reception that followed.

Some daughters and sons find the committal to be the most demanding ritual. Herbert Anderson and Edward Foley accurately conclude, "The act of committal is a stark and powerful expression of separation."[23] *Committal* is the right word. We "committed" Mother into God's care. Later, I found great comfort in the words of Madeleine L'Engle: "God, if he is God, if he is worth believing in, is a loving God who will not abandon or forget the smallest atom of his creation. And that includes my mother. And everybody, everybody without exception."[24]

## THE FUNERAL WAS A DISASTER!

Not every son or daughter is always pleased with the funeral. When Maud Powell died in 1984, her son Colin was stunned by the absence of the familiar in the liturgy at Saint Margaret's Catholic Church in South Bronx.

> The modernists had taken over. All that had meant so much to me, the imagery, the poetry, the liturgy, had been changed . . . . The present young priest at St. Margaret's had taken modernism to the extreme, rendering God genderless and ordinary. I knew my attachment to the forms of the past was more emotional than intellectual. But I found it disconcerting to discover that the rock of faith I was raised on could move. My mother

received a unisex, low-key, non-triumphant burial service. I do not recall hearing the word "God" mentioned once. I found myself whispering, "Don't worry, Mom. We'll do something better later, because this is not the way you would want to go."[25]

## Music

One of the ways we make a ritual special is in the selection of music, particularly music that was a mother's favorite. Liza Minnelli chose "The Battle Hymn of the Republic," which her mother had sung at John F. Kennedy's funeral. Although her siblings, Lorna and Joey, wept, Liza stood "serene and dignified" during the song.[26]

When my friend Dorothy Culver died, her daughter Nancy wanted to use the Purdue University Fight Song, because "Dot" had lived all but the last three of her ninety-three years in West Lafayette, Indiana, home of Purdue. Just before she died, learning that her beloved Boilermakers were going to the Rose Bowl, Dot sang a spirited rendition of the fight song. Nancy hesitated. "I don't know if it would be appropriate for a *church* funeral."

"Do it, Nancy," I urged. So in the First Christian Church, after the minister's benediction, we burst into smiles as the organist enthusiastically played the Purdue Fight Song. A Boilermaker was going home.

## Remembering

Sometimes, children remember little of a mother's funeral. Howard Clinebell recalled, "I remember nothing the minister said at my mother's funeral, but I recall with appreciation that he put his hands on my shoulder as he left the funeral parlor after the services."[27]

Richard Nixon rarely expressed his emotions in public. His mother had witnessed his defeat for the presidency in 1960, and for governor of California in 1963. Just before Hannah Milhous Nixon went into surgery, Nixon, "at a loss for appropriate words had told her, 'Mother, don't give up.'"

"Richard," she responded, "don't *you* give up. Don't let anybody tell you you are through."

When the funeral for his mother, his most loyal supporter, was over, Nixon walked out of the East Whittier Friends Church overwhelmed by his loss. When he shook the hand of Dr. Billy Graham, who had conducted the funeral, "the tears broke loose. He put his head on Graham's shoulder and sobbed. Only he knew how lucky he had been to have Hannah Nixon for a mother, only he could guess at how much he owed to her."[28] In little more than a year, Nixon would be elected president of the United States.

## THE BURIAL

Going to what Thomas Lynch calls "that hole in the ground" can be sobering. No matter how much we try to camouflage the grave with artificial grass and flowers, it still is a hole in the earth that mirrors the hole in the heart. For some, the cemetery is too final, too brutal. Lynch, a funeral director, poet, and essayist, accepts no excuses.

And you should see it till the very end. Avoid the temptation of a tidy leave-taking in a room, a cemetery chapel, at the foot of the altar. None of that. Don't dodge it because of the weather. We've fished and watched football in worse conditions. It won't take long. Go to the hole in the ground. Stand over it. Look into it. Wonder. And be cold. But stay until it's over. Until it is done.[29]

Even humorists have to face the sobering finality of a mother's funeral day as syndicated columnist Lewis Grizzard discovered:

We buried Mom on her birthday, October 3. She would have been seventy-seven. We took Mama down to the little cemetery and put her next to her own mother. In the last year Mama often would become confused and would ask relatives where her mother lived. "She's dead, Christine," somebody would reply.[30]

Now, Grizzard's mother was dead, too. Dead and buried. Weather can be a big anxiety for grieving children. Who wants to stand under a tent and watch a mother's casket lowered into a muddy grave? Bill Tammeus and his three sisters and their families did that. It had been raining for days in rural Illinois but, as Bill's mother would have pointed out, the "air was the kind of noticeable clean it gets only after a serious rain scrubbing."

> So there we were, four orphans saying farewell to their old mother under a spring-blue dome of sky. Fresh flowers did their important work of beauty on the casket. But flowers, too, soon fade and blow away. And the truest thing I can think to say about all this now is that the world simply works this way. And no one—not even an orphan with three orphan sisters—can change that.[31]

Sons and daughters in such moments, in James Wall's words, need "the presence of others, we need the presence of God, to stand with us in grief."[32] It was wonderful that friends and family were "with us" at the visitation and at the funeral, but I needed familiar faces as I read my mother's committal. Andy and Gwen Morgan had driven from Chicago, Eric Fruge and James Stillwell had driven from Lexington, Andy Baker and Karl Babb had rearranged schedules to be a companion to a friend as he buried his mother. How do you adequately thank such kind people? It takes more than a card supplied by the funeral home.

We finished singing, "And When the Battle's Over We Shall Wear a Crown." The spirited singing ricocheted off the marble mausoleum walls. In that moment the world of eternity and the world of earth intersected in that space. God stood with us that February morning fulfilling his promise to "bind up the broken-hearted" (Isa. 61:1).

## WHO COULD BE HUNGRY?

After the committal, the ladies of the church had prepared lunch for the family. Ironically, although some children do not feel like eating after a funeral or memorial service, sons and daughters find themselves gathered around tables in a church hall, a restaurant, or a home. Like sitting around a mother's table, such a gathering can comfort even in her strong absence.

> Thousands of meals around this table,
> Mom interrupting her own plate to ask,
> (seemingly every five seconds)
> "What can I pass you?" or
> "Now eat up, there's plenty."
> Even after we were full, Mom would say,
> "I don't want any leftovers."
> Could I ever forget
> "Not until you clean your plate . . ." moments
> I can hear her ask, "Anybody need anything?"
> Yeah, Mom, there is something I need—you!

Many eat, or at least sample, the donated food gifts. Some imbibe. Frank McCourt reflects: "You'd never know from the way we ate and drank and laughed that we'd scattered our mother who was once a grand dancer at the Wembley Hall and known to one and all for the way she sang a good song."[33]

> I've eaten the Colonel's chicken before
> but it never tasted like it tasted
> today in a church gymnasium
> when family and friends gathered after the services.
> Different in a way I cannot explain.
> I would have sworn
> "Who can be hungry at a time like this?"
> But when one of your mother's friends has prodded,
> "You need to eat something . . .
> let me fix you a plate"

to be polite, I ate the food she placed in front of me.
     All of it.
Sometimes, it is "comfort" food—
     the food you've eaten a thousand times before
     memory-evoking food, whether potato salad, cole slaw,
     coconut cake.
Sometimes, just by tasting,
     you know which one of your mother's friends
     made the green bean casserole or congealed Jell-O salad.
In a real way, this gathering around a folding table,
     covered with a plastic tablecloth that will
     be tossed into the trash afterwards,
     becomes something of a Eucharist.
You can't sit around talking long
     because the youth are coming to play volleyball.
Soon their exuberant joyfulness
     will drown out the residue of the grieving
     family who ate potato salad and fried chicken.
I suspect that the next time I bite into
     a fried chicken leg, well, at least one from the Colonel,
     I will remember that chicken leg.


How would daughters or sons survive the rituals without so many kind people?


I walked into the church kitchen
     to thank the ladies
     who had interrupted their plans for the day
     to prepare a meal
     for their friend's family.
Almost embarrassed, they responded,
     "We were just glad to do it . . ."
     Then someone added, "We thought a lot of your mother."
Standing there, I realized Mom had once been part of
     the prepare-a-meal-for-the-family brigade.
Mom had often been summoned,

"Mary, can you bring potato salad and something sweet?"
The commercial has it right:
"Nothing says lovin' like something from the oven."

Although a grieving son or daughter may have no appetite, Howard Clinebell writes, "The meal after the funeral affirms the ongoingness of life in spite of the loss. Eating together becomes a kind of communion meal—a way of saying, 'We can and must go on, together.'"[34]

This meal they prepared
became an elegant eulogy
that I will long remember.
They expressed sorrow by being servants to a grieving family.
They know, sooner or later,
their sons, daughters will sit at these same tables
and someone will feed them.

## THE NUMERALS

After a second helping of desserts, we drove back to the cemetery where two hours earlier we had left our mother. Because flowers are not allowed in the mausoleum chapel, the floral gifts lined the sidewalk. My sister, brother-in-law, and I avoided the confrontation with the four numerals—1999—that had been so recently added, by looking at the flowers.

"Mother would have loved the flowers," my sister commented. I agreed. Because the cards had been removed so we could send thank-you notes, we had difficulty identifying who had sent what. "Seems a shame just to leave them . . ." but I could not imagine funeral sprays in my room at the Holiday Inn.

My mother was buried in a crypt next to my father, second floor by the south window. For eleven years, her name had been on the marble—but not her life range. Now, the numerals on the marble leaped out at us like pulsating neon: Mary C. Smith, 1916–1999.

My parents owned cemetery plots before they owned a home. "First things first," they reasoned. As my father lay dying, however, my mother drove by the cemetery on a cold, rainy day. The wet cold convinced her it would be "awful to put your father into a hole in the ground in the rain." She exchanged the plots for two crypts. That was the first major decision my mother ever made.

I'm not sure how long we stood taking it in, but we eventually walked around to see if we recognized any new names. Finally we drifted out to rethink the events of the day in our own minds and hearts.

## Where Do We Bury Mom?

Not all parents plan for their own burial place. Some children face a difficult decision on where to bury Mom. When Judy Garland died in 1969, one of her former husbands wanted her buried in California; her children, Liza, Lorna, and Joey, rejected the idea, knowing how much she loathed California. Although Garland's will stipulated cremation, Liza ignored the directive and buried her in New York, even though the burial had to be delayed until a spectacular crypt was finished a year later.[35]

The burial can be isolating even when you are standing in the presence of family and friends. Lynn noted of her siblings, "We were together, but alone in our experience of loss." At her mother's grave, she realized, "We had never talked about our mother before and were not about to talk about her then."[36] No two siblings, not even identical twins, grieve alike. Siblings honor different slices of memory. While writing this book, there have been moments I have had to call my sister to ask questions to jog my memory.

I have come to believe that memories keep grieving sons and daughters returning to the cemetery. Across the landscapes of our lives, some daughters and sons have posted "no grieving allowed" signs. But a cemetery offers a safe place to remember.

## Mourning in the Limelight

Finally, the two sons had privacy. Their mother's death had touched off a media frenzy. An estimated two billion people had watched these boys walk behind her casket. The cameras had captured the flowers with the ribbon inscribed, "Mum." On a worldwide level, it was described as "one of the largest outpourings of grief in modern times." But for William and Harry it was a premature good-bye to their Mum, Diana, "the people's princess."

During the service in Westminster Abbey, the boys had not cried until Elton John sang. (Few saw those tears because Queen Elizabeth had forbidden cameras to focus on the boys during the service.) Now, like millions before them in less remote cemeteries, they stood at a mother's grave.

> It was late afternoon, and gathering clouds threw shadows across the emerald lawns of Althorp. William and Harry stood, hands folded before them, stared at the flower-draped coffin as the final prayers were said. Then, as Diana was slowly lowered into the freshly dug grave, the rays of the late afternoon sun suddenly sliced through the clouds and fell on the casket. Tears flowed freely down the faces of Diana's sons as they, and the rest of the family, were overcome with emotion.[37]

The sons walked back to their mother's childhood home. There, like other grieving sons and daughters, they ate with the family. Although heirs to the British throne, that afternoon William and Harry were grieving adolescents like so many others who have grieved an early death.

> A son, daughter, whatever age, leaves a cemetery changed.
> You may have been there before
> but this time changes you.
> You have buried your mother!

## RECOGNIZING YOUR ORPHANHOOD

On a February day, my friend Brenda Atkinson stood in a South Carolina cemetery talking to the friends who had attended the funeral and who had accompanied the family to this sacred space. Through all the "Bless your heart's" and "I'll be praying for you's" one thought kept darting into her mind—not necessarily menacing, but bearing more reality than she wanted to deal with at the moment. Brenda turned to her sister-in-law and whispered, "I'm an orphan."

"What?"

"I'm an orphan now."

Linda, her sister-in-law, thought a moment before answering, "Yes, you are." For several years, Brenda and her mother had shared a home. So much of her life had been organized around noticing and meeting the needs of her mother. Now, her own needs would dominate as she began trying out orphanhood. And one of those needs was to grieve well.

## CREMATION

The growing acceptance of cremation means that sons and daughters are no longer locked into a seventy-two hour window for committal (although many Jews bury within roughly twenty hours, sundown the next day after death, unless it happens to be a Sabbath). Reversing the order, cremation before a memorial services gives people time to rearrange schedules and to make more informed decisions in planning services.

There may be a memorial service—with or without the cremated remains (the preferred term). Some are not ready to give up the ashes of a mother. Some want time to select the right place; after all, you cannot re-scatter ashes. Scattering is permanent.

Gaining possession of the cremated remains can be sobering, as a woman named Kelly discovered:

> I was stunned when I received my mother's cremains. I simply answered the door, and there stood the UPS man. "Package for you." "What is it?" I asked. "Probably something you ordered," he

said and dashed back to the truck. It was only after I opened the outer package that I gasped: This was my mother! Or should I say, what was left of my mother. I would have thought there would have been more of her. Mother had sent me things via UPS. I didn't know that your mother could show up in a UPS truck!

Dorothy Gallagher describes the initial "temporary" committal of her mother's remains:

I put my mother's ashes on the floor of the closet, right next to my shoes. I left them there from December until March. In March, a year after my father's death, I bestirred myself. I called the funeral parlor where I had abandoned (not too strong a word) his ashes. I wondered how long they kept uncollected cremains. . . . My father's cremains were still on the shelf, so I collected them, and one day in early spring I took a trip up to the house with my cousins and two boxes of remains.[38]

For some sons and daughters, not scattering or interring the ashes is a way of postponing the final reality of a mother's death. Families argue over disposition of a mother's ashes or custody of the cremated remains, alienating other family members. Custody of cremated remains is increasingly a subject of litigation. Liz's three siblings teamed up against her, promising to let her know when they would scatter their mother's ashes. They never did. To her sisters, it was about settling an old feud with mother's favorite. "I have no where to go on Memorial Day, or Mother's Day, or Christmas, or the days I simply miss her," Liz laments. "How could they have done this to me? I am their sister."

## Taking Mom Home

The McCourt brothers honored their mother's wishes to be "reduced" and buried in the graveyard at Mungret Abbey, outside Limerick City in Ireland. One August day in 1985, Frank, Malachy and his wife Diana and son Cormac, and Frank's fourteen-year-old daughter, Maggie, gathered with neighbors from boyhood and with friends from New York. In a ritual other sons and daughters have experienced,

> We took turns dipping our fingers into the tin urn from the New Jersey crematorium and sprinkling Angela's ashes over the graves of the Sheehans and Guilfoyles and Griffins while watching the breeze eddy her white dust around the grayness of their old bone bits and across the dark earth itself.[39]

Yet their hearty Hail Mary "wasn't enough." Although the McCourts had drifted away from the church, they later realized that they would have received comfort and dignity from the "prayers of a priest, proper requiem for a mother of seven."[40]

## GOING HOME

Finally, we had fulfilled our responsibilities. We had buried mother. Now, it was time for me to go home to Kansas City. My sister worried aloud about who was going to look after me. I reminded her that I was now, in fact, a "big boy." Had I not proven that by conducting my mother's funeral?

One of the floral tributes from my friend Richard Gilbert came in a mixing bowl, not unlike the one in which my mother had made biscuits thousands of mornings. "How will you get it on the plane?" my sister asked.

I wrapped the arrangement in a garbage bag and tied a large knot so I could carry it. When the airport security guard asked, "What's in the bag?" I undid the knot and pulled the plastic down so that the flowers and the bowl were visible.

"What beautiful flowers!" she said.

"They are from my mother's funeral. I buried her yesterday."

"I will pray for you," the security guard whispered as she helped me rewrap the bag. I walked toward my gate hoping that she would remember. In the days ahead, I will need the kindness and the prayers of strangers as well as friends.

The plants did not survive my skills as a gardener, but the bowl is perfect for popcorn. That bowl reminds me of the kind friends who offered comfort to a newly motherless child.

## A Prayer

God, I am alone, motherless.
Alone feels more intense than I imagined.
　Stand with me in this place. Amen

# 5. THE GRIEVING

*Prince William is not a little boy. He cannot grieve forever. He must learn to take it.*
—Faculty member at Eton[1]

*Our society has little tolerance for grief. We expect it to be discreet, tidy, and above all, short-lived. Memorial services, burials, wakes . . . are appointed occasions for expressing loss and grief. Once these rites have been completed, the survivors are supposed to grieve privately and be done with as quickly as possible.*
—Victoria Alexander[2]

*The more I think about it, the harder it is for me to get everything done. I just try to put it to the back of my mind, pretend it didn't happen.*
—John Law[3]

*There was no longer anyone who would ever again claim me as their child. No longer was anyone living who had been present at my birth, who had witnessed my first steps, heard my first words, walked me to my first day of school, or paced the floor, nervously, the first time I borrowed the family car. No one knew the details of my life and my family's history. I was no longer anyone's child.*
—Alexander Levy[4]

Do you recognize a universal expectation in the Eton tutor's words, "He cannot grieve forever. He must learn to take it"? Our culture has little tolerance for a son or daughter who for months, or even years, later is still grieving. Mourning is the initial level of a long learning curve. Grief is the permanent residence of our hearts.

> At times I feel like a parking meter.
> Time is up!
> No one feeds the meter for me.
> There are individuals who negatively comment on my grief.
> "Still grieving, hey!"

The word *still* is one of the ugliest words in the vocabulary of grief. It can often singe when used by those who don't "get" grief. But how could they understand? Their mothers are alive! Some want to believe that if I can get over it expediently—then, when their turn comes, they will, too. Alan D. Wolfelt writes:

> Sometimes you'll hear about mourners "recovering" from grief. This term is damaging because it implies that grief is an illness that must be cured. It also connotes a return to the way things were before the death.
>
> Mourners don't recover from grief. We become "reconciled" to it. In other words, we learn to live with it and are forever changed by it.[5]

Not everyone grieves openly. One's grief is shaped by several influences: the nature of the relationship with the mother, the circumstances of the death, the adult child's personality, cultural background, support system, spirituality, and gender.

> I have been telling myself
>     that I am fifty-one years old!
> Decades have passed since I resided under her roof
>     and lived by her rules or depended upon her.

## SETTLING THE ESTATE

In some families, settling an estate can come months, even years after a mother's death. Some siblings find dividing up the possessions to be torturous. Sometimes, there are the possessions that no one wants, those that necessitate an estate, yard, or garage sale. The estate sales trouble some daughters and sons. The days leading up to a sale can be agonizing and, depending on the number of possessions, it can take a lot of work to organize, display, and price items. What price do I put on my mother's things? For one daughter, the sale day was emotionally exhausting.

> I couldn't believe the attitudes of people who showed up. One woman just breezed in and said to her companion, in a loud voice all of us could hear, "This is just junk! They should have hauled this stuff to the dump." Then there were the people who didn't want to pay the price we had put on it. After about the third person asked, "Would you take less for this?" I was ready to pack it all up and go home. You would not believe how cheap some people can be—wanting something for nothing.

Timing is to estate settlements what location is to real estate. My friend Nancy did not have a choice. Her brother was off work and could drive down and "get it all done." So on Christmas Eve, they emptied their mother's apartment in a retirement community. "It had to be done, but I wasn't ready. What a way to celebrate Christmas—getting rid of your mother's stuff."

On the other hand, settling an estate can have an element of humor. Nancy Keller, in an E-mail sent sixteen months following her mother's estate sale, writes: "I just received the legal papers Friday to close out Mom's estate." Nancy added one word that needs little explanation to estate-settlers: *finally*.

> It feels very good to get the "paper work" out of the way. I leave in an hour to meet my brother, Jim, halfway to Michigan. We plan to meet at a McDonalds to give him his check for half the estate. I said it will be like a drug deal. Sitting in the back booth

saying, "Did you bring the money?" Ha. Jim said, "Now we can supersize our order!"[6]

## HOME AS AN EMPTY HOUSE

The difference between a home and a house is in the memories of the children who grew up there. Dorothy Gallagher described walking through the family home one last time:

> We walked through the dark, dismal rooms. Except for the sour smell of decay, everything was gone: clothes, furniture, books— none of it good enough for the Salvation Army—had been thrown into a dumpster by men wearing gloves and surgical masks. Here, under the kitchen windows, was where the table stood, covered with its stained plastic cloth.[7]

When I read Gallagher's experience, I recalled mine. My sister had asked if I wanted to walk through my mother's house one last time before the new owner got the keys. I had always known it was a small house—I did not realize *how* small. How had eight of us lived for a while in a two-bedroom house? Without the familiar, the house seemed alien. I looked to the "marker" places where familiar items had been as long as I could remember. For example, the clock above the stove. Missing! In the living room, the pictures of two birds—gone! The wall clock in the living room—not only was it gone, but the nail hole in the wall had been plastered over. The hall closet was empty. That's where you could always, *always* find fresh towels and washcloths. On those cold winter nights before we had central heat, you could find another blanket or comforter. But now that closet was empty— completely cleaned out.

I felt sad backing down the driveway that last time. We had moved in just days before my sixth birthday. Somewhere in my possessions is a picture of a skinny blond kid sitting on the front porch holding a birthday cake with six candles and a Hop-a-long Cassidy satchel. I remembered all those times when I backed down the driveway leaving for college or for my own home with mother standing and waving good-bye.

While doing research in the Truman Presidential Library, I found a letter that Judge Jed Johnson had written Harry Truman following Mother Truman's death. "Having lost my own mother several years ago, I know that going back home has never been quite the same without her."[8] As a son, I immediately recognized the accuracy of Judge Johnson's insight.

> Someone now lives at 4809 Beech Drive.
> I have no idea their names or any of their details of their family.
> To me it will always be Momma's house.
> How I miss having Momma's house to go home to.
> 4809 Beech Drive was not just a house—
>     it was home.
> But in time, it will become the remembered home
>     to the children who now live there.
>     And on some distant day they will walk
>     through that house one last time
>     and remember a mother
>     who made it home.

## TELLING OUR STORIES

Sometimes we cannot mourn because we get caught up in spinning our narratives. Mae Gleason, mother of comedian Jackie Gleason, died when Jackie was a teenager. Over the years, as Gleason became more famous, he reworked the narratives of his mother's death the way he honed jokes in his comedy routines. Gleason's stories were constructed to project the image of a self-made man. His popularity as Ralph Kramden in *The Honeymooners* only increased the appetite of fans for biographical snippets. In one version, "the orphan" left his mother's funeral and headed to Manhattan with only thirty-six cents in his pocket!

Gleason remained furious for the rest of his life with anyone who posed [questions]—as, doubtless, he remained furious with himself for having failed to live in a way that could enable him to answer them comfortably. In the absence of a bearable truth, he invented a lie, the biggest and most self-excusing of his life, and the one he told most consistently and often.[9]

Gleason "reduced by as much as six years, in some conversations, how old he was when his mother died" making "himself a schoolboy . . . or even a Dickensian urchin of thirteen." He told one reporter that he had been exactly "fifteen years, eleven months" when his mother died. The reporter checked the date on Mae Gleason's tombstone. How could Gleason have been so misleading?[10]

What Gleason did on the grand scale, others do on a lesser scale. Sometimes siblings have difficulty helping each other grieve because recollections and memories are so different. My mother frequently admonished us, "If you can't say something good about someone, then don't say anything." In researching this book, I reached "dead ends" with some subjects because they offered only passing mentions of a mother's death in their autobiographies.

*Mother's Day*
How can it be Mother's Day?
    You are not here.
You are not here to receive my card.
    I am an orphan.
You are not here to receive my gift.
    I am an orphan.
You are not here to receive my hug.
    I am an orphan.
You are not here to hug me back.
    I am an orphan.
Yet, you are here!
    Along the corridors of my memory
    you bake and wash,
    bathe and touch,

scold and question,
comfort and soothe.
So, today, while many celebrate Mother's Day
at brunches and dinners
I will wander through my memories
remembering how you mothered me.

## GRIEF DURING A HOLIDAY

A mother's death does not have to be recent to be felt on a holiday. Just hearing "I'll Be Home for Christmas" can challenge my emotional control. It may be "beginning to look like Christmas," but it doesn't feel like Christmas. Harry Truman could not face going home to Independence, Missouri, for Christmas 1947, five months after his mother's death, because it brought back too many memories. So he invited all the Truman family to come to Washington, D.C., to celebrate at the White House.[11] Although he was president of the United States, during those days of Christmas he was Martha's boy Harry.

Others found the second or third Christmas without mom more challenging; in some cases, they were numb during the first. Some feel a fresh sense of loss every Christmas.

## FORGIVING

Some individuals blame themselves for a mother's death, especially when a mother died in, or soon after, childbirth. What was life like for Alice Roosevelt, whose mother died two days after birthing Alice? Biographer Edmund Morris described Alice as a nineteen-year-old orphan "haunted by the ghost of [her mother], hurt by [her father's] denial of that ghost."[12]

H. W. Brands, another Roosevelt biographer, charged that Teddy could not think of Alice "without thinking of her mother, especially since there was a growing physical resemblance between mother and daughter." Because his mourning for his wife was "barren and incomplete," Roosevelt "shut up and shut off those feelings, speaking and writing almost nothing about them."[13] Historians long believed that Roosevelt had destroyed every letter from Alice's mother as well as every picture of her. Brands speculated, "At some level he probably blamed baby Alice for her mother's death. Consciously, of course, he would have resisted any such bald formulation. . . . Yet at a deep emotional level he understood that if not for the baby, the mother wouldn't have died."[14]

Years later, Alice noted that she had been hurt by his refusal to tell her anything about her mother. "He never mentioned my mother to me. He never even said her name." It is no surprise that Alice Roosevelt would conclude in her diary, "Father doesn't care for me. . . . That is to say, one eighth as much as he does for the other children. . . . Why should he pay any attention to me or things that I live for, except to look upon them with disapproval."[16] I believe Alice grieved throughout her whole life.

Sometimes, because of our post-death and post-ritual fatigue, it is easy to blame ourselves for real or imagined offenses. Lots of children have screamed (or thought), "I wish you were dead!" Not only do you remember the words—siblings also remember them. Although friends and family long witnessed our devoted caregiving and attention, we cannot forget.

Grieving offers an invitation to forgive and to receive forgiveness. Some daughters or sons find it easier to forgive others than to forgive themselves, thinking, "I should have . . ." or "If only I had . . ." If I have someone to blame for a mother's death—doctors, God, even myself—it makes the death easier to deal with. In time we must forgive lavishly and generously. Jeanine Bozeman blamed her sister-in-law for her mother's death. Years later she confessed,

> Little progress has been made toward forgiving my sister-in-law, and I do not really want to forgive her. I would like to conclude by saying, "I'm working on it," but I probably am not. Perhaps I feel I will be betraying mother or being disloyal to her if I forgive her. Maybe being unforgiving is an effort to "keep Mother alive." I am not sure, but I often think about it.[17]

## Awaiting a Grief Ambush

Some attempt to keep "tight reins" on their grieving. If so, it hides out somewhere in the body waiting for the right moment to ambush. Grief has an impact on every system of the body. One reason grief for a mother is so complex is that it is our longest relationship. Alexander Levy reminds grievers:

> We begin our life as an embryo attached to the wall of our mother's womb. It's our first relationship. Not much in the way of interaction but, quite literally, a vital connection. We are dependent on an umbilical cord for nutrients and oxygen, on a sack of fluid for warmth and safety. This is our first interpersonal experience.[18]

But it is more than just biological attachment. Levy, like many, initially dismissed the orphan title. "I didn't particularly 'feel like an orphan.' . . . I didn't feel 'like' anything at all. What I felt was afraid."[19] Wait a minute, Levy. You are a psychologist! What is this "afraid" business? Readers can picture the panic he experienced as a child shopping with his mother when he realized she was no longer behind him. "I remembered that panic so clearly, when I ran up and down the aisles screaming, 'Mommy. Mommy.'" Unfortunately, Levy mistook another woman's legs in a skirt for his mother. Years later, he has not forgotten the woman's comforting words, "What's the matter, Honey, have you lost your mommy?" Standing at his mother's grave, he felt the same sense of loss. If any of his mother's friends had asked that question, "I could have begun sobbing then, too."[20]

I was surprised reading Levy's account, on the eve of the third anniversary of my mother's death, having the same memory. I vividly remembered losing my mother in the women's section of J. C. Penney in downtown Louisville. I was too short to see over the racks, and my panic was immediate, loud, and profound. As I write this, I am surprised by the surge of panic I experienced that day a half-century ago.

## FINDING MYSELF

For actress Goldie Hawn, the defining moment in her grieving occurred months after her mother's fatal heart attack in November 1993.

> When my mother was alive, I was the daughter first and everything else second. . . . That's what made her death so painful. My mother was a big part of my life and a big reason why I did what I did. I've always derived a lot of energy from being a good daughter. . . . When she was gone, I suddenly thought, Why am I doing this? For whom? Losing my mom was really hard on me. I remember going to the Academy Awards shortly after she died and thinking, Well I'm all dressed up, and my mother won't see me.[21]

The world expects a daughter to get on with her life after a period of appropriate grieving. But who defines "appropriate"? Hawn cleared ample emotional space for her grieving and discovered what many sons and daughters discover: "In a large sense I turned a page in my life when my mother passed on. I realized that all the things I was doing were simply not enough."[22]

For more than two years, Hawn did not work. After exploring Indian and European spiritualities, she came to the sobering conclusion that she had never been taken seriously. She was known as laughing Goldie—a million laughs. During those years out of the limelight, Goldie later wrote, "I was coming to terms with death and what it is all about."[23] Ending her seclusion following her mother's death, Goldie announced a radical restructuring of her production company and fired her agent—actions that stunned Hollywood. Some quickly attributed the decisions to an overreaction following her mother's death; however, in Goldie's mind, "It was simply time to take control of my life. My mom used to say 'Goldie, you've got to do it yourself and stop depending on other people.' My mother's death was a big passage for me."[24]

Many readers recognize the wisdom in Hawn's words: "My mother's death was a big passage for me." Millions of children—

regardless of the age—have concluded, "I will never be the same again." For some, a mother's death turns into a "developmental push" that "may effect a more mature stance in parentally bereaved adults who no longer think of themselves as children."[25] Singer Patti LaBelle said so accurately, "A girl never really becomes a woman until she loses her mother."[26] Nor does a boy become a man.

Some of us avoid the small things that we need to do as part of the grieving process. Tomorrow—I will do it tomorrow. I procrastinated throwing away a single rose from my mother's casket spray.

> I really should do something with this dried pink rose
>     lying on my desk.
> It has not moved in the months
>     since I brought it home from Mother's funeral.
> I laid it on my desk until I could find
>     a better place to put it.
> But, if I move it—now—
>     from this place,
>     it will seem out of place.
> One rose plucked from the casket spray
>     has strangely comforted me.
> My mother loved roses.
> My mother grew beautiful roses.
> She still loves roses.
> I bet she is still growing them!

I cannot remember when I threw away the rose.

## FINDING GUIDANCE

Some grievers find guidance in the experience of others. As I have read the biographical materials included in this book, I have repeatedly said: "I wish I had read this when Mother first died." During the years I have listened closely to grievers who have participated in my Grief Gatherings. I am still looking for tips to surviving the terrain called grief.

There is no buzzer that goes off announcing the end of griev-ing. Leo's mother died when he was two; his father died when he was nine. The next year, his grandmother, his surrogate mother, died. Then at age thirteen, he lost his two aunts who had cared for him. Life was difficult especially during adolescence. At age sev-enty-seven, he wrote in his journal:

> Felt dull and sad all day. . . . I wanted as when I was a child to nestle against some tender and compassionate being, and weep with love and be consoled . . . become a tiny boy, close to my mother the way I imagine her. Yes, yes, my Mama (whom I was never able to call that because I didn't know how to talk when she died). . . . Mama hold me, baby me![27]

This motherless griever, Leo Tolstoy, wrote the masterpieces, *War and Peace* and *Anna Karenina.* If Tolstoy can grieve over a life-time, so can I.

"But doesn't time heal?" some protest. Isn't that the advice so freely dispensed to individuals struggling long after a mother's passing? Jeanine Bozeman responds, "Time heals, I often hear. I will never be cured of my sadness, but I have been changed by it. I shall be richer all my life for this sorrow."[28]

Here's what I have come to believe:

Grief will not have the final word.
No way!
There will come a distant dawn
    when I realize grief has not won.
That indeed grief has only been a companion
    on a portion of the path.
And I will be wiser for having
    made room on the path.
Life has a way of surprising grievers.

So, the next time someone suggests that you should be over your grieving, just reply, "I am doing thorough grief." They probably will not know how to respond to that and will move on to another topic.

## HEAVEN

My motherloss has been tempered by my nonnegotiable belief in afterlife. I love the way James Kavanaugh expressed hope: "I believe in a life that lingers after this, a life that God has fashioned for his friends."[29] While I cannot explain the details of the eternal life my mother believed in and that I have come to believe in, I trust Jesus' words, "If it were not so, would I have told you that I go to prepare a place for you? And if I go and prepare a place for you, I will come back and take you to myself, so that where I am, there you may be also" (John 14:2-3).

> During these grief-filled days
> I hold tightly to one nonnegotiable belief:
> I will see my mother again.
> While I do not understand all the details of the promise
> I do believe in the One who made the promise.
> In those moments when I feel
> ambushed by grief, again,
> I am comforted by Jesus' promise
> to "go away and prepare a place"
> Jesus can be taken seriously.

I believe I will see my mother again. I expect to again hear those familiar words, "Oh, Honey, I'm so glad you've come." I am not alone in entertaining such thoughts. When Kirk Douglas was hospitalized after a massive stroke, he wondered, "Could I see my mother again? I would like that."[30] I have read and reread his words, "Oh, how I would like to thank her for all of the things that I never thanked her for."[31]

Just as my mother took my hand as a child and led me on the big adventure of exploring downtown Louisville, on some distant day, she will again take my hand, and lead me on the big adventure of exploring heaven. In the language of the Eternal Town I will, at last, find adequate words to thank her for loving me so lavishly.

## ANNIVERSARY GRIEF

I am reminded this day, attending a convention in California, that it is not just any day on the calendar of my heart. It is the real mother's day: the day my mother died. So, I got up early to spend some time with the grief that shows up on anniversary day.

Thankfully, years ago, I discovered that the "five stages of grief" is only a helpful theory—woefully inadequate to wrap around motherloss (or any loss). Today I will give my grief permission to hang out with me. I will not snarl, "Leave me alone." I will probably not tell anyone that this day—February 21—is my mother's resurrection day. Three years ago today she found out how true Jesus' promised resurrection is. I have been encouraged by the opening of Alexander Levy's book, *The Orphaned Adult*:

> Twice a year, once in the spring and once in the fall, on the anniversaries of my parents' deaths, I travel to the cemetery on the other side of town. Once there, I kneel beside the carved stone beneath which lie their remains, and I tend to the few small plants growing there. I don't go there to garden. I don't go there to visit my parents, either. There's nothing of them there. . . . It is a place I go to spend time with memories. I'll sit a while and wonder about many things, especially about the strange experience of having become an orphan as an adult.[32]

I am glad I found Levy's book a week ago. The experienced grief of this griever gives me permission to make special this day. So, although three thousand miles from the mausoleum, in my imagination, I will make a trip I have made before. I will drive through the twisting lanes of Louisville Memorial Gardens and park. I will punch in the security code and climb the steps to the second floor of the mausoleum. I will walk the marble to that familiar space. And there I will spend time with the memories. For a while I, too, will wonder about many things, especially about the ever-learning experience of becoming an orphan at midlife.

## THE LESSONS THAT GRIEF TEACHES

As an author, I wish my mother could read this book. I still find myself wanting her to be proud of me. I remember so many afternoons riding the yellow school bus with some treasure I had made at school. Something that would cause her to stop what she was doing, wipe her hands, hold the gift in her hands, turn and look at me and say, "Honey, this is so nice. You did a good job. I am so proud of you."

I don't dare disclose this when I lecture. I fear that someone would explode: "Oh, for heaven's sake, grow up!"

I will grow older. I will grow old, perhaps. But I will never grow up—not if that means abandoning my need of a mother. Not if that means sidestepping the lessons that grief would teach me.

My mother's death was not a tragedy
    just the predicted conclusion of a long, well-lived life.
Nevertheless I keep reminding myself
    that I have to be the "big boy"
    my mother always wanted me to become.
But my soul keeps interrupting
    to tell me that, in midlife,
    I feel, at times, like I did as a child
    in moments in the night
    when I cried out, "Momma!"
And she came and brought enough comfort
    to convince me that no monsters
    lurked beneath my bed.
I must remember all those times
    she told me that there was no bogeyman
    trying to get me.
Unless motherloss is the ultimate bogeyman.

# A PRAYER

Lord, I do not know how long
   this season called grief
   will last.
But you do.
I trust you to accompany me
   on an unfamiliar path
   as you have accompanied
   others. Amen

# 6. THE REMEMBERING

*But first and foremost, I remember Mama.*
   —John van Druten, *Three Comedies of American Family Life*[1]

*Having lost my mother, I've gone through life with the pain of an amputated limb. The pain of a limb that has been sawn off, but that remains in the severed nerve, in the scar tissue. A phantom pain. . . . After she died, I was adrift and a familiar unreality settled in me.*
   —Alba Ambert[2]

*I found that with time I actually feel my mother's presence in my life more than ever. As I go through different stages of my own life, I talk with my mother and know that she is with me. I really think that I am closer to her now than ever before.*
   —Sally Higgins[3]

*I miss Mom, and I am finding a place for her in my life even though she is not physically present.*
   —Michelle Windmueller[4]

THE MINISTER OF THE CHURCH I attended as a child was enamored by Abraham Lincoln's words: "All that I am, or hope to be, I owe to my angel mother."[5] Every Mother's Day—and many Sundays in between—he would weave Lincoln's quote into his sermon. Nancy Hanks Lincoln died when the future president was nine; his father soon married Sarah Johnson. Historian Benjamin Thomas wrote, "Abraham adored [Sarah]. Recollection of his own mother dimmed. In later years he called Sarah, who filled her role so well, 'my angel mother.'"[6]

Many sons and daughters struggle with remembering. How do I love or care for a stepmother, or a live-in, without dishonoring the memory of my birth mother? One man remembers:

> My dad just walked in one day with this woman . . . maybe three months after my mother died and announced, "This is your new mother." I didn't want a new mother and I certainly didn't want to call her "Mother" or "Mom." But my father threatened, "Boy, either you call her 'Mom' or I will knock some sense into you." Well, let's just say he attempted to knock some sense into me on several occasions. Finally he quit trying. That woman never became "Mom."

No few "new" wives have battled a husband's children from a previous marriage or marriages. No few husband-fathers have gotten caught in the cross fires of relational stress. In some cases, a title has to be arbitrated. Acceptance of that title and the person generally takes time—lots of time, sometimes a lifetime. While some children graciously transfer allegiances, others recognize a stepmother the way citizens in underdeveloped nations recognize de facto governments.

## "Just Call Me 'Mother'"

Alice Lee Roosevelt died in February 1884, two days after giving birth to her namesake, Alice. Following her baptism, the baby's father, Theodore, handed Alice to his sister Bamie to raise. In 1887 he married Edith Carow. After a long honeymoon in Europe, when the newlyweds returned to New York, the new Mrs. Roosevelt insisted that the three-year-old Alice live with them, although Theodore preferred continuing the old arrangement. Edith's insistence that Alice call her "Mother" confused the child because Aunt Bamie had taught her to pray for her mother "who was in heaven." Alice felt like an outsider in her father's new family.

Edith wounded Alice with derogatory comments about Alice Lee: "If Alice Lee had lived . . . she would have bored Theodore to death."[7] Alice, a strong-willed child, sought unsuccessfully to gain her father's attention in outrageous ways (including keeping a pet snake in her bosom).

Years later, after an elegant White House wedding to Congressman Nicholas Longsworth, Alice turned to thank her stepmother. Edith cut her off. "I want you to know that I'm glad to see you go. You've never been anything but trouble."[8]

## Mother's Circle

Many sons and daughters learn to allow another to share "mother's circle." Others, verbally or mentally, angrily snarl, "You're *not* my mother!"

After writer Alba Ambert's mother died, he lived briefly in Puerto Rico with the woman who had raised his mother. But his father abruptly took Alba to New York City to live with his own mother, Alba's grandmother, who wanted a chance to raise a child (she had abandoned Alba's father). Alba recalled:

> My grandmother despised her sons' wives. This disdain was not reserved for the living. It included *la difunta,* the deceased, as she called my mother. She called me *la huerfana,* the orphan. She objectified my mother and me and treated us as less than human. But I held on to whatever I possessed of my mother when I was commanded to call my grandmother Mami, forcing me to negate the existence of my real mother, whose presence must have been very much alive in my mind.[9]

The grandmother's demands had consequences: "Compelled to call someone else Mami, forbidden from talking about my mother, I became adept at all things hidden. I turned into a silent child and learned to keep my feelings tucked away in a deep recess where no one could violate them. In this way, I lost my mother again."[10]

For many adults, the first person you call with good news is your mother. In the great moments of life, we want to call and say, "Hey, Mom, guess what?" Readers will remember calls to announce an engagement, or getting the great job, or the "I can't believe it!" promotion. I wonder if Nobel Prize and Oscar winners call home, too, with the intensity of athletes grinning into a camera and waving, "Hi, Mom!" Now there's no mother to call.

I loved to hear the Lettermen sing,
    "We will have these moments to remember."
Life may be able to "take away" my mother
    but life cannot take away my memories.
Often I slip a memory disk
    into the video player of my mind
    and take a seat in the theater
    which has space for only one.
And I remember. I remember Mama.

## CREATING THE CHERISHABLE MEMORY

Denman Dewey believed that one element in healthy grieving is creating a "cherishable" memory.[11] Without denying any of a mother's mistakes or negative qualities, a son or daughter can choose to stop rehearsing the wrongs, or hunt for the slightest good to remember. For two thousand years, grieving children have found guidance in the words of Paul, "Whatever is true, whatever is honorable, whatever is just, whatever is pure, whatever is pleasing, whatever is commendable . . . think about these things" (Phil. 4:8). Tom Attig builds on Paul's wisdom, saying, "Consciously remembering those who have died is the key that opens our hearts, that allows us to love them in new ways."[12]

Sometimes we must remember a mother in new ways before we can love her in new ways. If we create a cherishable memory, our mothers will be easier to carry into our futures. Creating a cherishable memory is not unlike creating a work of art or a quilt. It requires sitting in the quiet of a beach or a park or woods and giving oneself permission, "I want to remember the time Mom . . ." or "I *choose* to remember how Mom always . . ."

> In the "scrapbook of our mind"
> there are some snapshots we put toward the front,
>     some we place toward the back.
> Some pictures we choose not to include.
> It is, after all, my album of memories.

Some will need a safe place or space, a workshop in which to fashion, over time, a cherishable memory. Browsing in an antique store, I discovered a print of a royal family in a battered cheap frame. After making the purchase, I removed the print from the battered frame.

"You don't want the frame?" the owner asked.

"No, keep it." When I took the print to a specialty frame shop, I was complimented on my find. Barbara Bartocci writes: "Today, in my home you will notice the reframed, well-framed print." One task for some grieving sons and daughters is to "reframe" unpleasant memories of mother, especially when, as Barbara Bartocci notes, "Memories of my mother *tangled* in my mind like multi-colored strands of thread."[13]

> Part of my mourning is not "hanging out"
> with memories of the last years of mother's life
> as dementia reeked havoc.
> I am not ignoring the memories.
> I am not afraid to go there.
> I just don't stay long if
> I am summoned by a particular painful memory.

## WHEN GRIEF IS SABOTAGED

Alba Ambert writes: "I've always felt that I've lived two parallel lives, like the rails on a railroad track. One is the life I have lived since my mother died. The other is the life I would have lived if she were here."[14] For some, working with memories is demandingly painful. Some families have worked hard to create a favorable "public" image—nothing must tarnish, including certain realities about a mother. Some are taught that a good son or daughter "keeps" the secrets.

Grieving can be complicated and even sabotaged by unresolved issues with family members. Sometimes, grievers do not focus on a real person but on an idealized mother. But grieving offers any son or daughter the chance to remember realistically. Edelman addressed the issue:

> From an early age I received the subtle cues that told me never to speak out against the dead. The sanctification process following a mother's death is one that surpasses the rigor of any church, elevating all subsequent mention of her to the most laudatory and idealized heights. Because we loved them, because we wanted them to be flawless when they lived, we honor our mothers by granting them posthumous perfection, and we soothe ourselves by creating the mothers we wish we'd had.[15]

## WHAT DO YOU REMEMBER ABOUT YOUR MOTHER?

Dagoberto Gilb remembers "holding her hand at a train depot. I can still feel my arm in the air, limp and soft with trust. It must have been Union Station, Los Angeles, and I don't know where we were going or why. I was thrilled. I was small, probably just walking, and looking up at her. I knew then she was beautiful."[17]

Joyce Maynard remembers a telephone number: "I still remember my mother's phone number, even though it's been more than twelve months since I've dialed it. . . . But even now there are times when I have a wild impulse to call her and tell her some piece of news. It takes a second to remember nobody's there."[17]

Red-letter days on the calendar stimulate remembering. Edelman writes:

> Birthdays also activate grief responses, not only because they remind us of the phone call or card that never comes but because each one we celebrate brings us closer to the neon number: the age a mother was when she died. Because we identify so strongly with our mother's body, and because our fate was once so intertwined with hers, many of us fear that the age of physical demise will also be our own. To reach the year is a milestone; to pass it becomes one of our most glorious achievements.[18]

Remembering well can be demanding work for a daughter or son. Although you think that there are things you could never forget, over time, details grow hazy. Like light bulbs, memories come in different wattages: 25, 50, 75, 150. Some memories brighten and go dim like a bulb on a dimmer switch. For many, a memory is like a bulb that gradually dims and goes out.

Sometimes we forget because our memories are like underexercised muscles. Blessed are those who have siblings or friends who can "jump start" the memories. "Don't you remember when Mom . . . ?" Or "How could you forget the time your mom . . . ?" Mothers are not dead until we stop telling stories about them or repeating, often to a new generation, "My mother always said . . ."

Stories are like scarves pulled out of a magician's fist. You never know what is tied to the next ribbon. Remembering may be all we have of a mother's existence. Alba Ambert writes:

> Nothing concrete or tangible exists of her. Not even a photograph. She was buried in a potter's field, so the simple consolation of pressing my finger against her name on a tombstone is unattainable. If I had not been born of her and lived to remember, it would be as if she had never existed. When I die, she will cease to be.[19]

Laura Scott, an editor for the *Kansas City Star,* worries about the lost stories and traditions of past generations of family members.

> I remember many times my mother talking about all of these women, and what she remembered about them. My children need to know, too, about the people of the past who have impacted their young lives, for each family is a reflection of the experiences and values of its preceding generations. Like my mother, I will tell the family stories to children who aren't always eager to listen. And hope that when their turn comes, they will remember them.[20]

## A WARMING MEMORY

Thorough grief requires remembering. We dance with the memories, sometimes leading, sometimes following. As I look out at the ice and snow from my vantage point in the medical school library at Kansas University, I remember past winter nights. After a snowy day we would make our way home in the dark to the back door, stomping snow off, wiping noses on our sleeves, and stepping into the steamy kitchen. Mother would say, "Now go wash your hands. Dinner is almost ready."

This cold Friday night, I wish I could walk into my mother's kitchen and know a good dinner was moments away and again hear Mom ask, "Did you have a good time?"

I remembered Mother last night as I made my way through a darkened house hunting for a kerosene lamp. My mother believed in keeping kerosene lamps and flashlights handy. In fact, she would have been astonished at my lack of preparation for this winter storm. How, I asked myself, could I have forgotten this life lesson from Mom?

Memories are summoned by snippets of song, book titles staring out from shelves, television shows (how many Bob Hope specials did Mom and I enjoy together?). Memories are summoned by a scent, a smell, a taste, a touch, a word, a sound. I acknowledge that reality when I browse in antique shops. I hear myself say: "My mom had one just like that. Wonder what happened to it?"

Some grievers have memories that stand out.
Memories that are rewound and replayed,
over and over again become
cherished memories.

Paul McCartney cherishes this memory of his mother:

My mum, as a nurse, rode a bike. I have a crystal-clear memory of one snow-laden night when I was young at 72 Western Avenue. The streets were thick with snow, it was about three in the morning, and she got up and went out on her bike with the little brown wicker basket on the front, into the dark, just with her little light, in her navy-blue uniform and hat, cycling down the estate to deliver a baby somewhere.[21]

## THE TOUGH MEMORIES

Not all of our memories are warm. A few menacing memories may appear slightly out of focus. Others have a museum of memories. Choose a category and press "Start tour here." Some scan their memories, always looking for fresh evidence that will lead to a grand jury indictment of a mother.

The same event may be remembered and interpreted differently by siblings. Remembering accurately is an essential element in grief. Some view memories through a lens that distorts the memory like the mirrors in a carnival fun house. Some of us take seriously our role as family "rememberer" or preservationist.

In Jewish culture, the word *hesped* is a call for a balanced memory despite the adage, "Speak no ill of the dead." *Hesped* says there is wisdom in creating a balanced memory of Mother. I once asked participants in a group to name one thing they remembered about their mothers. A woman spoke up, "Flatulence." I thought I had misunderstood. She repeated herself, "Mom always prided herself on her ability to fart. And she always seemed to have a lot of gas."

The thorough griever needs to cultivate some good memories. It may be brief, but there has to be something positive. It is important to grieve the real mother rather than a fictionalized one. Eleanor Roosevelt, whose mother was heartless to her, remembered watching her mother dress for social events in New York City's high society. "I was grateful to be allowed to touch her gown or her jewels."[22]

Daughters and sons have, over time, reconstructed a more positive memory of their mothers—some only after an encounter with a stepmother from hell! I laughed at a T-shirt in a shop in Estes Park, Colorado, which read: *I Have Issues*.

> It's not the "precious memories" remembering that bothers me.
> It's the "unprecious" remembering.
> The ones that re-boot so much more vividly.
> The memories that leave little bruise marks on the soul.
> The memories that dart in and implode!

Edelman reminds us:

> Every human relationship is affected by ambivalence, every mother an amalgam of the good and the bad. To mourn a mother fully, we have to look back and acknowledge the flip side of perfection and love. Without this, we remember our mothers as only half of what they were, and we end up trying to mourn someone who simply didn't exist.[23]

## REGRETS

Some sons and daughters indict themselves with lists of regrets and "I should have's." This morning, unaware that I would be writing on regrets, I meditated on a phrase from *The Book of Common Prayer*: "by what we have done, *and* by what we have left undone."[24] Ask me about the tyranny of the undones. I can grill my heart like a veteran prosecutor. Did I visit Mom enough? When I visited, did I stay long enough? Was I patient with Mom? Could I have done "more"?

I lived five hundred miles from my mother. I did not have the option of "dropping in" after work or dinner. As a grief educator, however, I have listened to countless anguished stories of sons and daughters wrestling with regrets that stir up my own regrets. Although I am not a priest, I receive anguished confessions. I grant absolution—certainly not the type a priest would offer, but the kind humans compassionately dispense over a cup of coffee.

I often respond, "If your mother were listening to this, what would she say to you?" Levy, an adult orphan, provides this insight: "Although it is often called 'guilt,' in the conventional language of grief, it seems to me that it really is more a type of regret—either that we did not do more when we had the opportunity to do so or that we did not get the opportunity to do more."[25]

Some daughters and sons have done too much "more" and have negated their own health, jobs, and relationships. A few want you to know how much they sacrificed while siblings shirked their responsibilities. One man told me:

> My sister was always scheduling me for guilt. I hated that nursing home! You couldn't get five feet in the door before the scent of urine smacked you. But it was what we could afford. My sister was there all the time. She might as well have moved in and slept in the other bed in the room. She had lots of ways of letting me know that I wasn't pulling my share of the load. "Oh, don't worry about me . . ." I admit, that toward the end, I stayed away. I just couldn't watch Mom deteriorate, die. I couldn't take it.

Some feel torn by competing loyalties, like the woman who said:

> I tried to be Super Daughter, Super Mom, and Super Wife. By the time Mom died, I was a crazy woman. At a soccer game I was on the phone checking on Mom or talking to her social worker. At the nursing home I was on the phone talking to my daughter going home from soccer practice. I fell apart when Mom died. I didn't know what to do with myself. My whole life was organized around Mom's care.

Sometimes, long after rituals are over, grieving children revisit their decisions: If I had it all to do over again, would I do it differently? The dying and death of this man's mother certainly inspired that question to be asked:

> I regret that I ignored my own family, including my wife. I couldn't do enough for Mom, which meant I didn't do enough for my wife. At times, I was a walking zombie. Lovemaking? You've got to be kidding! So, she looked elsewhere for attention and affection. The day after we buried Mom, she said, "I've met someone. . . . I want a divorce."

## In Unexpected Moments

Grief-linked memories erupt in unexpected moments. Sitting in Branson, Missouri, in a hotel ballroom, I waited to speak at a conference while Stephen Hill, a Nashville musician, "warmed up" the audience. I reviewed my notes, unaware that I was singing along. Stephen was closing his set with the old gospel song "Beautiful Isle of Somewhere," one of my mother's favorite "heaven" songs:

> Somewhere the sun is shining,
> Somewhere the song birds play
> Hush then thy sad repining
> God lives and all is well.[26]

Suddenly, I was not a middle-aged man, but a young boy sitting on a church pew next to his mother on a hot summer Sunday night. Watching her sing, occasionally her finger pointing to the flow of the stanza. During the week, my mother would often sing heaven lyrics as she washed, cooked, ironed, and cleaned.

As the choir or a quartet sang, it was not uncommon to see my mother mouth the words that offered her so much hope of a future life. My mother could not have theologically explained heaven but could sing dozens of songs with themes of heaven, many of which we sang to her that last week as she dodged death's embrace: "How beautiful heaven must be," "The holy hills of heaven call me," "I'm bound for that city on the beautiful shore," and "Land where we'll never grow old."

> Never grow old, never grow old.
> In a land where we'll never grow old.
> Never grow old, never grow old.
> In a land where we'll never grow old.[27]

Oddly, early this morning, facing a long day working on this manuscript, I awakened hearing "Beautiful Isle of Somewhere" in my mind and heart. In my grief, I have come to a renewed belief in the promise found in the songs that my mother sang. In moments when my intellect questions the reality of eternal life— or at least some dimensions of it—I sing the heaven songs I learned from my mother.

## A Remembering Party

When Nancy Keller moved to Goshen, Indiana, two of the first friends she made were Jan and Anne. During the years, the trio celebrated the births of their children and mourned the passings of their mothers. One Mother's Day, when Jan's mother was in the hospital with terminal cancer and Anne's mother was critically ill in another hospital, Nancy was acting as a nursemaid to her ninety-two-year-old mother who had fallen at the retirement center.

> That Sunday night of Mothers' Day, I called my friends at the various hospitals where they were keeping their death watch. I suggested that we all take a break and honor our mothers with a few hours off to regroup and recharge. I remember how we sat in the South Side Soda Shop huddled together in a back corner booth sharing our stories and our sorrows. We stayed until closing. They had to ask us to leave. Both Jan and Anne's mothers died shortly after that evening. My mom lived another year and a half. (We voted her most likely to survive that night.) We were

there for each other at the funerals, the cleaning out, and the ever-dreadful garage sales that break your heart.

The trio has also been there for the important work of remembering. "We are still there for each other on those days that you just need to share a story or a memory. They understand."[28]

## Remembering Mom on Thanksgiving Eve

This Thanksgiving Eve I am struggling with memories of a dozen other Wednesday nights before Thanksgiving. In college, graduate school, after my divorce, there was something about pulling into the driveway in Louisville late in the night. Home. My mom always waited up. The kitchen was warm and filled with the delicious aromas. Regardless of the time I arrived, my mother would ask: "Are you hungry? Do you want something to eat? It won't take me a minute to fix you something." Some of those "somethings" would leave Martha Stewart panting for the recipe. Mom always assumed the answer to the first question would be yes. After unloading the car, I found myself sitting at her kitchen table eating and talking with her.

There is no home to go to this Thanksgiving Eve. I miss Mom.

## Biscuits

The most ordinary incidents can stir up "serious" remembering.

> Eating breakfast in Beaumont, Texas,
>     I had no idea that I was in for a memory moment.
> I had bitten into a biscuit—
>     not the assembly-line, factory produced,
>     but a genuine homemade biscuit,
>     which tasted like those my mother had made
>     on several thousand mornings.
> The more I savored that particular biscuit
>     the more I remembered Mother's.

I almost expected her to nudge me,
    "Better hurry . . . don't want you to miss the bus."
How could one biscuit taste so wonderful?
Why didn't I learn to make those biscuits?
I suspect it's more than the recipe—
    because most of my mother's recipes
    were remembered deep within her
    although the rudiments could be found
    on a file card somewhere.
Having a recipe for biscuits—
    would be like having a recipe for oxygen.
That morning in Beaumont, I ate one biscuit after another.
I miss her biscuits.
My mom will never make me biscuits again.
Unless they have kitchens in heaven
    where mommas can make biscuits
    for recently arrived sons and daughters.

And then there were my momma's Gumdrop Cookies. Now please don't get me started on those Gumdrop Cookies.

Rose Marie Mansfield remembers her mother's canning skills. Damson plums are not good to eat, but make wonderful preserves, especially when eaten on her mother's "mouth-watering" biscuits. Rose Marie assumed that when her mother moved into the retirement home, that would be the end of the preserving. Then came a call from her mother, "Bring me a dozen pint jars and ten pounds of sugar."

Rose Marie quickly figured out what her mother was up to. On her mother's floor was a tiny kitchen. Under the cover of night, Rose Marie made the delivery. Her mother, then age eighty-five, and her accomplice, Irene, age ninety-five, were going to make preserves! Both had heart conditions, cataracts, were hard of hearing, and used walkers. Rose Marie found herself anxious about how this adventure would end—probably a summons for a "chat" with the administrator. The next afternoon as Rose Marie stepped off the elevator, she smelled damson preserves.

I rounded the corner to see the girls, purple stains and sticky syrup covering most of them and all the tiny kitchen. Worn out but laughing and glowing with pride, they showed me their jars of preserves. They had to rest now, and would clean up later. We untangled walkers and they rolled off to their rooms to rest. I went into action, which was part of their plan. I cleaned all the purple, burned-on, sticky jam in the kitchen before the other residents woke up from their naps. Having restored the kitchen, I gathered my things and left, knowing that this was not the end. Figs would be ripe in a few weeks.[29]

Six years after her mother's death, Rose Marie wrote me, "This is one of my favorite stories about her."

## LEGACIES

Ruth Bell, born to missionary parents in China, is the wife of Billy Graham. One of Mrs. Graham's fondest memories is the way her mother stood by Ruth's father in troubled times in China, particularly during the Japanese occupation during World War II. From her mother, Mrs. Graham learned the art of what she called "gracious good-byes." Dr. Bell often traveled to remote villages to offer medical care and was gone for long periods of time.

> Even though each time Billy left for a crusade it felt like a "small death" (as I once wrote in a poem), the good-byes were much easier because I'd seen my mother having to say so many good-byes—not only to her husband but to my sisters and me when we went away to high school in Korea and then on to college in America.[30]

Sometimes one particular memory stands out, often a last memory that was a parting gift, although unrecognized at the time. Colleen Townsend Evans remembered, "God used my mother to teach me to have fun—not as a separate event but as an integral part of all the work, the responsibility, and even the agonies of parenting." One day, after a great meal with Colleen's family and four children,

> she walked with us to the car. As we said our hasty good-byes and fastened our seat belts, she stood by the curb, lifted her tailored suit above the knees and did a fancy little jig. Our teenaged children, who absolutely loved their Grandmother Mimi, roared with laughter. As we pulled away from the curb, my mother, still dancing her jig, called, "Hey, hey! Not bad for an old girl, eh?" That's the last memory my children have of their grandmother on this earth. Not bad, Mom . . . indeed, not bad at all.[31]

Liz Curtis Higgs remembers that the last time she saw her mother alive was on Mother's Day. Liz's father had brought her home to die surrounded by the things and people she loved, particularly her garden. Liz's sister Sarah had spent a day weeding and cleaning up the portion of the garden that could be seen from their mother's bedroom window. Liz vacuumed and cooked "a dreadful dinner" of burned hamburger steak and overdone green peas. "She loved it. She even ate it."[32]

Small things reactivate our loss. Mary Jensen remembers: "I miss the way she routinely ended our phone calls with, 'Bye, Honey. I love you.' I miss the way she scratched my back when I was little—and not so little. I miss having someone interested in anything and everything I have to say."[33]

Have you found your mother's words tumbling out of your mouth and groaned, "Now, I am beginning to sound like my own mother"? Kathy Troccoli's mother was known for funny phrases like "Well, it's all fun and games until someone gets hurt!" and classic admonitions like, "Money doesn't grow on trees." Sound familiar?

> There are many phrases my mother used to say when I was growing up. Some of them I still laugh about with friends. My sister and I often remind each other of those bold "words of wisdom" she would often quote to us. But in the last years since Mother's death, I have come to be comforted by those very phrases.[34]

## THE MEMORIES THAT SHAPE US

Johnnetta Cole writes: "The woman who bore me is no longer alive, but I seem to be her daughter in increasingly profound ways."[35] The same is true of sons. Memories have a way of shaping us. In our lives come inevitable moments that remind us whose child we are—or have been.

Sue Bender, author of *Plain and Simple* and *Everyday Sacred,* was asked to record these books for audio publication, a project that would require a week of her time. The taping, unfortunately, proved to be more difficult than Bender had anticipated. Repeatedly she heard, "Cut. Can we try that again?" After a full day in the studio, only twelve pages had been recorded. Bender left the studio discouraged. At home she complained to her son, David, "I don't think I'm good at this kind of storytelling."

"One of the fondest things I remember about Grandma," David began, "is how much I loved how she read stories to me. I always looked forward to it."

"I took his words in, really heard what he had to say. I took a deep breath and felt those famous indicators, my shoulders, which are often up close to my ears, drop down as I thought, 'Maybe I am *my* mother's daughter.'"

The next day Bender "read from my heart, envisioning the way my mother had read."

"What happened last night?" the director quizzed her. Bender remembered her mother.[36]

Sometimes, we as grievers need to borrow someone else's remembering to stimulate ours.


## ACTIVE REMEMBERING

Some adults have difficulty remembering the date of a mother's death; for others, there is no way to forget it. Paul McCartney's mother, Mary, died on Halloween 1956, when the future Beatle was fourteen. He would remember his mother in the lyrics of his ballad, "Let It Be," which was a result of a dream a decade after her death. He also put her picture, wearing her nurse's uniform, on the cover of his first solo album.[37] Many grieving sons and daughters cherished the words of "Let It Be," remembering their mother's "words of wisdom." Some long to spend time again with their mothers.

I have a strategy for remembering. I go through the memory bank and deliberately remember one of the good ones, like the days I spent with my mother on a spring vacation. We stayed in a house built in 1828 in Pleasant Hill, a Shaker community. The beds were high off the floor. All night I worried about my mother becoming confused, rolling out of bed, and breaking a hip. (Try explaining such an accident to the siblings!) The next morning when I awoke, my mother inquired, "How did you sleep?"

"Oh, so so." I responded.

"I didn't sleep so well either," she answered. "I was worried about you falling out of bed and breaking a leg and how I would find someone to help me." Then I told Mom about the fears that had kept *me* awake, and we had a good laugh. The next night we slept on beds at the Hampton Inn that ensured sounder sleep. Writing this, I smile at a "good" memory. It was the last vacation my mother took. That memory is a "keeper."

## A Prayer

God,
Help me remember to remember.
Help me forget to forget.
Make me a wise steward
of the capacity to remember.

# 7. THE HONORING

*Honor your father and your mother, so that your days may be long upon the land.*
　　—Exodus 20:12

*One of life's greatest regrets is not being able to give her all the things that I could if she were alive today.*
　　—Jack Welch[1]

*No matter how we struggle to be wholly separate, no matter how far away we plant ourselves, we are destined to exist in relation to our mothers, to the very source of our lives. Our achievements are their achievements. Our failures are their failures. Our dreams are only variations of those our mothers dreamed for us. We reject their expectations, or strive to live up to them, but we live our lives forever in the shadow of theirs.*
　　—Joie Davidow[2]

*There never was a woman like her. She was gentle as a dove and brave as a lioness. . . . The memory of my mother and her teachings were, after all, the only capital I had to start life with, and on that capital I have made my way.*
　　—Andrew Jackson[3]

IF SOMEONE HAD DEPOSITED A DOLLAR in the bank for every time my mother resorted to Exodus 20:12, I would have quite a nest egg. Of the thousands of verses in the Bible, my mother wore this one out: "Honor your father and your mother, so that your days may be long upon the land." She skillfully wielded that verse. She seldom said, "You had better listen to me, young man!" No. She dragged in my grandmother, "If I had talked to my mother the way you talk to me! I shudder to think . . ." And Mom dragged God into the issue, "You know what the Bible says: 'Honor father *and mother* that your days may be long upon this earth."

Years later, while riding the London subway, I repeatedly heard the continuous warning, "Mind the gap!"—the gap between the floor of the train and the floor of the subway platform.

> It can be a demanding task, at times,
>     to mind the gap,
>     to reconcile the mother before
>     and the mother after
>     some seminal event.
> It can be demanding to reconcile the frail woman I visited
>     at the nursing home
>     with the robust mother of my childhood.
> I began grieving years before
>     as the "frailing" began.
> I cannot exactly pinpoint the day
>     I began grieving.
> Rarely could I acknowledge that grief
>     because it felt like treason.
> I felt, at times, like one of those characters in movies
>     who kill their mother
>     so they can get their inheritance.

My mother always put herself down because she only had an eighth-grade education. That was one reason she dreamed of a college education for me. "Don't be like your mother," she repeatedly told me. After she died, I thought about ways to honor her. Then my alma mater created a program to initiate scholarships using installment payments, although the scholarship would not be awarded until it was fully funded. I began writing checks to the university. Someday there will be the first recipient. Having a scholarship named for her would have brought an embarrassed smile to my mother's face; in fact, I suspect she knows. I do not think the distance between eternity and earth is great. I believe there are punctures of reality in heaven's atmosphere that allow mothers to know our efforts to honor them.

## WAYS TO HONOR A MOTHER

There are as many ways to honor a mother as there are sons and daughters.

✣ Give your grief its voice. Find ways to express your loss.

✣ Display photographs of your mother. Justice Ruth Ginsburg of the U. S. Supreme Court keeps a picture of her mother in her office.

✣ Reframe some old pictures. At holidays, bring out special pictures that are holiday-related. Have an old or tattered picture restored.

✣ Donate to a worthy cause in honor of your mother. The amount of your donation is unimportant.

✣ Donate a book in her honor to a library. Choose a subject that would have interested her, or request that the money be used to buy resources on mothering.

✣ Name a child or urge that a grandchild or great-grandchild be named for your mother. Unfortunately, in our culture we never added "junior" or Roman numerals after a mother's name—but we should have.

✣ Remember the best advice from your mother: "Eat your vegetables. Stand up straight. Don't talk with your mouth full. Slow down. Go to bed. Wash your hands." Many of those admonitions still make sense.

✣ Visit or revisit places your mother loved. If you cannot physically go there, look at pictures or videos of the area or think of some memories.

✳ Donate a poinsettia in honor of your mother to an organization during the holidays.

✳ Do a mitzvah, or good deed, in honor of your mother.

✳ Attend a community service honoring mothers on Mother's Day.

✳ Watch some of your mother's favorite movies.

✳ Use your mother's china or glassware for special meals.

✳ Plan ways to pass on your mother's possessions.

✳ Remember your mother on All Saints' Day (November 1) or All Souls' Day (November 2).

✳ Organize a photo album of pictures of your mother. You may want to do an overall album or focus on a particular period or theme of your mother's life.

✳ Revisit the old neighborhoods.

✳ Save something your mother owned to pass on to grandchildren or great-grandchildren.

✳ Write a biography of your mother. If you have difficulty, use this as an opening sentence: "I will always remember how my mother . . ." or "I will never forget the time my mother . . ."

✳ Write a poem about your mother. Try this sentence to begin the creativity: "I never realized that my mother could . . ."

✳ Refinish a piece of your mother's furniture. For years, my mother's cedar chest was in my home. But, in settling the estate, her bedroom suite went to one of my nephews. It seemed right that the chest be reunited with other pieces of the furniture that had been in my mother's bedroom for a half-century.

✳ Make a collection of your mother's "mom-isms"; for example, "Well, as I live and breathe . . ." or "She's a bird . . ." or even "If that don't beat the cats a-fighting!"

✳ Do a "stretch" gift of generosity. As I was writing this book, I attended an estate sale and found two elegant bronze sculptures of children. My initial impression was, "Oh, wow." I noticed the price tag (about the expense of a trip for a family to Hawaii). My alma mater had just completed a new library. As I admired the bronzes, I mused, wouldn't it be something to donate those sculptures to Trevecca in honor of my mother? Today those two bronzes are in the entrance to Waggoner Library with this plaque: "In honor of Mary Catherine Eckert Smith and all the mothers who sacrificed so their daughters and sons could have Trevecca educations." Hopefully, down the road, some current students will remember this act and find a way to honor their mothers.

🌿 Become a companion to someone who is newly experiencing motherloss. A cup of coffee, a movie ticket, or even a phone call could be an invitation to help them sort through their feelings.

🌿 Compile something of your mother's; for example, recipes, poems, or sayings. You don't have to be Caroline Kennedy to put together a compilation of your mother's favorite poems, but as a start, use *The Best-Loved Poems of Jacqueline Kennedy Onassis* as a template. You could make this collection of poems into a calendar, selecting one poem or quotation each month. Invite family members to write originals as well. Caroline Kennedy writes: "One of the greatest gifts my brother and I received from my mother was her love of literature and language. Sometimes knowing that someone else liked a certain poem can cause us to take another look at it, puzzle over why they might have liked it, and before we know it, be captivated by it."[4]

🌿 Create a "mother's" calendar honoring your mother. Use photographs, artwork, her favorite quotes, or sayings. These make valued gifts of remembrance.

🌿 Reset some of your mother's jewelry; thus, a diamond ring could become earrings or a brooch.

🌿 Put some of your mother's letters or notes on a computer disc. Letters are wonderful to hold, but over time may be misplaced or become illegible.

🌿 Listen to your mother's favorite music.

🌿 Organize a remembering "party" for family members. My friend Nancy Keller organized a wonderful "Let's celebrate our mothers" on Mother's Day.

🌿 Plant a tree or bush in honor of your mother. Watch it grow.

🌿 Find a way to uniquely honor your mother on Mother's Day.

🌿 Complete a project your mother started. Alison McMillen completed a book of her mother's insights, which she self-published over five years. In 2001, St. Martin's Press picked up the work and published it as *When I Loved Myself Enough.* She writes: "I have a constant ache in my heart, a longing to see her again in this world. . . . Although I miss her terribly, I am comforted by the knowledge that, as this book is the truest expression of who my mom was, in its continued existence what she had to offer to the world will live on."[5]

⚘ Plan an informal gathering of your mother's friends. One daughter organized an annual outing and picnic at her mother's grave. Another daughter organizes an "I remember Mary Alice" luncheon each year.

⚘ Donate flowers in honor of your mother to a place of worship on a Sunday nearest her birthday, anniversary, or passing day.

⚘ Check on extended family members or friends who may be having a tough time with your mother's death.

⚘ Continue a tradition of your mother's; for example, an open house or a Fourth of July gathering.

⚘ Visit a favorite restaurant of your mother's. Why did she like this particular place? What was her favorite item on the menu?

⚘ Adopt one of your mother's good habits.

⚘ Explore your grief with a psychologist or counselor. Often a skilled outsider can ask the right questions that lead to real discovery.

⚘ Invest in someone's future in honor of your mother. This could even begin with buying a candy item from a student raising money for a band trip.

⚘ Take someone to the cemetery with you. Stories and memories have a way of "getting loose" when another person accompanies you.

⚘ Create something of beauty in honor of your mother. Wilma took her mother's clothes and made a beautiful quilt. I took my mother's gowns and robes and had them made into stuffed bears for members of the family.

⚘ Make a donation to your mother's alma mater.

⚘ Plan a post-death ritual (PDR) such as a gathering, a story-telling, or a party to be held weeks or months after the funeral. This informal gathering may be a setting in which friends of your mother will feel more comfortable.

⚘ Honor the life lessons you learned from your mother.

✣ Whenever you find yourself thinking, "My mother always said . . ." go ahead and say it. Remember that "I'm beginning to sound like my mother" is not always an indictment.

✣ Give yourself time to grieve. Ignore the pressures to "get over it" or "move on" with your life.

✣ Whenever you want to say, "Mom would have loved this," say it. This will give your children permission to say it after you are gone.

✣ Visit the grave or scattering area.

✣ Attend funerals of mothers of your friends. Your attendance and support will be appreciated.

✣ Donate money or time to an organization seeking a cure for the disease that claimed your mother. Remember it does not have to be a large donation.

✣ Compose a doxology of twelve things in your mother's life for which you are grateful.

✣ Write your will and end-of-life documents.

✣ Celebrate Memorial Day. For too many, this is merely the first day of summer rather than a day to remember our loved ones (even if you celebrated Mother's Day earlier in the month).

✣ Find a unique way to celebrate your mother's birthday.

✣ Give a copy of this book to a friend or someone going through motherloss. Underline quotes you think might be helpful.

✣ Cook your mother's favorite recipes. Make copies of the recipes to pass on to future generations.

✣ Join a grief support group. What you know about motherloss could benefit another person in the group or prepare someone in the group for her mother's loss.

✣ Organize an informal group to study *Grieving the Death of a Mother*.

✣ Give yourself and others permission to grieve. There is no timetable for "successful" grief. You probably already know this, but allowing yourself grief of your mother will give someone permission to grieve thoroughly for their mother.

✣ Be sensitive to children and adolescents grieving a motherloss. When you see a child grieving for a mother, remember that he or she may be a future Arthur Ashe, Lady Bird Johnson, or Hope Edelman.

✿ Pass on one of your mother's recipes. Several of my colleagues in the field of grief, Sue Berry (Jeannette Chaffee's Finish Summer Vegetable Soup), Saundra Straub (Viola Gikas Smith's Potato and Squash Delight), Ron Wilder (Dot Wilder's Mexican Cornbread), and Phyllis Rolfe Silverman (Mrs. Rolfe's Chocolate Cake), honored their mothers by contributing their mother's recipes to *Morsels and Memories,* the official cookbook of the Association for Death Education and Counseling. This honors our mother's greatest admonition: "Eat something."

✿ Remember the anniversary of another motherloss griever. Eleanor Roosevelt, one of the busiest women in the world, took time to write a note to her physician, David Gurewitch, on the first anniversary of his mother's death. Use Mrs. Roosevelt's words as a pattern:

> This time is sad for you but I hope also it brings you happy memories for that is as your mother would want it to be. She would want you to feel her love and her protective presence and she would rejoice in your growth. You probably do not realize it but you have grown in personal strength and power in this past year . . . the 28th must have some feeling of loss but this note and the flowers are to bring you a message of love and remembrance of your Mother and gratitude to her for what she was. . . .[6]

## A PRAYER

> God, for that for which I am grateful
> For that which, in time, I hope to be grateful
> For that which I am not yet ready to be grateful
> Enable me to find and to create gratitude
>     to honor
> this remarkable woman I have called Mom.

The Gumdrop Cookie recipe from my mother's collection:

Gumdrop Cookies
1 cup butter or margarine
1½ cups sifted Conf. Sugar
1 teas. vanilla
1 egg
2½ cups sifted all purpose flour
1 teas. soda
1  "  Cream of Tartar
1/4  "  salt.
1 cup small gumdrops sliced

Cream sugar, conf. sugar
and vanilla, beat in egg.
Sift together flour, soda,
Cream of Tartar & salt.
Gradually stir into creamed
mixture, mix well.
Shape dough into roll 2 in
in diameter & 12 in long.
wrap in wax paper, chill
several hrs or overnight
Cut 1/4 in thick slices,
place on un greased cookie
sheet. Decorate top with
gum drop slices, (Omit black,
Bake in 375° about 12 min.
or until lightly brown.
Cool slightly before removing
from pan. makes about 4 doz.

# CONCLUSION

*I found that I had to talk about my mother to everyone that I came into contact with during that first year. The more I talked about her and told people that she had died, the more comfortable I felt.*
  —Sally Higgins[1]

*The story of any one of us is the story of us all.*
  —Frederick Beuchner[2]

*Moms are not supposed to die. Moms are like bronze statues, around for a lifetime. Moms are like family heirlooms; they get handed down from generation to generation. Moms don't die. We still had too much to say to each other, too much to do together, too much more ahead. What are we supposed to do without you, Mom?*
  —Michelle Windmueller[3]

*Remembering is an act of resurrection, each repetition a vital layer of mourning, in memory of those we are sure to meet again.*
  —Nancy Cobb[4]

YOU'VE READ THE BOOK. NOW WHAT? Remember. Begin by telling your stories, even if you tell them only on the pages of a journal.

Be open to the moments when another's motherloss intersects with yours. Share what you are learning from your motherloss. If Claudia Taylor, Colin Powell, or Paul McCartney had told biographers "The subject of my mother's death is off limits," this book would have been duller because I would not have drawn upon their rich experiences. In time, opportunities to share your narrative and what you have learned about grief will find you. Someone will find what you know to be valuable for his or her grief path.

Engage your grief for your mother. A young college freshman named Hope attended a college that had a tradition of mothers calling daughters on Sundays. Long before there were phones in each dorm room, there was a phone in the hallway. Whoever answered would yell out, "Hey, _____, it's your mother!" Four years of Sundays reminded Hope of her loss. As did conversations before holidays, "What are you getting your mom?" and conversations after holidays, "What did your mom get you?" Mothers visited campus. Mothers mailed boxes of goodies. Mothers took daughters shopping. And mothers came for their daughter's graduations. Hope could not escape her mother's absence.

Hope could have buried these experiences but chose to engage the grief—to ask questions that launched a movement to recognize the reality of motherloss. This book could not have been written if Hope had not first written her classic, *Motherless Daughters*. Her experience and writing heightened public awareness.

What will you do with your grief? There may come the time that you decide you have a book within you. Your experience could offer insight to another griever. Someone who is so bereft will wander into a bookstore or library and find your wise counsel. Or it may be in a coffee shop, workplace break room, playground, or funeral parlor, where you share your experience with another.

Allow yourself to be changed by this loss. This is no little "blip" in your relational narrative. I have been forever changed by the death of my mother. I would not want to live unchanged by her death. I take life more seriously. It was a privilege to be her baby, her child, her son. When I read Liza Minelli's eulogy, "for the rest of my life I will be glad I was Judy Garland's daughter,"[5] I realized that for the rest of my life I will be glad that I was Mary Catherine Eckert Smith's son.

I believe in the communion of saints; in fact, the older I get, the more precious the concept becomes. I believe that when my resurrection day comes, part of the discovery will include seeing my mother again. She will not look like she did during those agonizing days of February 1999. She will be dazzlingly alert—herself.

Mom will know me. I expect to hear again, "Oh, Honey, I am so glad you have come to see me. How long can you stay?" However long I will wrestle with motherloss—the rest of my life—will seem as only a brief interlude as I answer, "Forever, Mom. Forever."

# NOTES

### Introduction

1. Laura Scott, "So Much Changes When Elders Pass Away," *The Kansas City Star,* 9 June 1995, sec. C, 5.
2. Joyce Maynard, "Liberating Loss Lets Happiness Be Personal," *The Oregonian,* 13 October 1990, sec. C, l.
3. Harold Ivan Smith, *Grieving the Death of a Friend* (Minneapolis: Augsburg, 1996), 9.
4. Jeanine Cannon Bozeman, "A Journey through Grief: An Analysis of an Adult Child's Grief in the Loss of a Mother," *Illness, Crisis & Loss* 7, no. 2 (1999), 91–9.
5. Hope Edelman, *Motherless Daughters: The Legacy of Loss* (New York: Addison-Wesley, 1994), 20.
6. Fergus M. Bordewich, *My Mother's Ghost* (New York: Doubleday, 2001), 3.
7. Ibid., 32.
8. George H. W. Bush, *All the Best: My Life in Letters and Other Writings* (New York: Scribner, 1999), 578.
9. Margaret Truman, *Harry S. Truman* (New York: William Morrow, 1973), 307.
10. Harry Truman to Dean Atchison, 29 July 1958, Truman Presidential Library.
11. Hendrik Booraem, *Young Hickory: The Making of Andrew Jackson* (Dallas: Taylor Trade Publishing, 2001), 110–11.
12. Victoria Alexander, *Words I Never Thought to Speak: Stories of Life in the Wake of Suicide* (New York: Lexington Books, 1991), 157.

### Chapter 1: The Dying

1. Laura Davis, *I Thought We'd Never Talk Again* (New York: HarperCollins, 2002), 3.
2. Venita Wright, *Velma Still Cooks in Leeway* (Nashville: Lifeway, 2000), 112.
3. Edelman, 97–8.
4. Malcolm Boyd, *Simple Grace: A Mentor's Guide to Growing Older* (Louisville, Ky.: Westminster Press, 2001), 39.
5. Bordewich, 321.
6. Thomas O. Chisholm, "Great Is Thy Faithfulness," in *Worship in Song* (Kansas City, Mo.: Lillenas Publishing, 1923), no. 86.
7. Reeve Lindbergh, *No More Words: A Journal of My Mother* (New York: Simon & Schuster, 2001), 28.

8. Cecil Woodham-Smith, *Queen Victoria: From Her Birth to the Death of the Prince Consort* (New York: Knopf, 1972), 417.

9. Barbara Bartocci, *Nobody's Child Anymore: Grieving, Caring, and Comforting When Parents Die* (Notre Dame, Ind.: Sorin Press, 2000), 26.

10. Mary Jensen. "Love Is Slow," in *A Tribute to Moms*, edited by Ruth Senter and Jori Senter, (Sisters, Ore.: Multnomah Books, 1997), 177–80.

11. Ibid.

12. Liz Curtis Higgs, "Lesson Unintended," in *A Tribute to Moms*, edited by Ruth Senter and Jori Senter, (Sisters, Ore.: Multnomah Books, 1997), 114-21.

13. Edith Kent, "Musical Finale," *Focus on the Family* 25:12 (December 2001), 24.

14. Bartocci, 25.

15. Dave Anderson, "A Grown Son, a Mother, and a Ceramic Goose," *Family Style* 6:4 (2000), 1.

16. Ibid.

17. Kirk Douglas, *Climbing the Mountain: My Search for Meaning* (New York: Simon and Schuster, 1997), 68.

18. Lindbergh, 84.

19. Bob Blauner, ed. *Our Mother's Spirits: Great Writers on the Death of Mothers and the Grief of Men—An Anthology* (New York: Regan/HarperCollins, 1998), 180.

20. Frederick Nenner, "A Mother's Voice," *Journal of the American Medical Association* 281:12 (1999), 1065.

21. Ibid.

22. Ibid.

23. Rebecca Morsch, conversation with author, December 1996.

24. Anna Quindlen, *A Short Guide to a Happy Life* (New York: Random House, 2000), 31, 33.

25. Larry McMurtry, *Paradise* (New York: Simon and Schuster, 2000), 75.

26. Ibid., 76.

27. Ibid., 158–59.

28. Ibid., 159.

29. Boyd, 43.

30. Mary Clare Griffin, *Language Lessons for When Your Mom Dies* (San Francisco: DayBue Publishing Ink, 2001), 9.

31. Ibid., 137.

32. Ibid.

33. Barbara Sherrod, "At the Well: Living with Dying—A Mother's Death," *The Other Side* 3:2 (March/April 2000), 42.

34. Ibid.

35. Stuart Nicholson, *Reminiscing in Tempo: A Portrait of Duke Ellington* (Boston: Northeastern University Press, 1999), 175.

36. Sherrod, 42, 44.

37. Ibid., 44.

38. Bartocci, 35.

39. Jane Ganahl, "Amy Tan Gets Her Voice Back," *Book* Issue 14 (January/February 2001), 44.

40. Ibid.

41. Ibid., 44.

42. Blanche Wiesen Cook, *Eleanor Roosevelt: Volume One, 1884–1933* (New York: Viking, 1993), 79.

43. Ibid.

**Chapter 2: The Passing**
1. Maya Angelou, *A Song Slung Up to Heaven* (New York: Random House, 2002), 77.
2. Edelman, xix.
3. Bozeman, 96.
4. F. J. Bowman to Harry S. Truman, 31 July 1947, Truman Presidential Library.
5. Bozeman, 94.
6. Ibid.
7. Ibid., 95.
8. Dorothy Gallagher, *How I Came into My Inheritance and Other True Stories* (New York: Random House, 2001), 35.
9. Jan Jarboe Russell, *Lady Bird: A Biography of Mrs. Johnson* (New York: Scribner, 1999), 53.
10. Lindbergh, 167.
11. Edmund Morris, *The Rise of T. R.* (New York: Coward, McGann & Geoghegan, 1979), 241.
12. "Star Gazing," *The Kansas City Star*, 2 May 1996, sec. F, 1.
13. "Man Allegedly Drag Racing Hits Car, Kills Mother," *The Kansas City Star*, 21 December 2001, sec. A, 14.
14. Bordewich, 13–14.
15. Ibid., 17.
16. Ibid., 20.
17. Ibid., 21.
18. Quindlen, 42.
19. "Siblings Have Little Time to Grieve Death of Parents," *The Kansas City Star*, 10 June 2001, sec. A, 4.
20. Pete Slover and Diane Jennings, "Farming Family Loses Mother," *The Dallas Morning News*, 6 May 1999, sec. A, 27.

**Chapter 3: The Mourning**
1. Russell, 53.
2. Kay Collier-Slone, "The Mystical Body," *The Advocate* 26:2 (February 1996), 3.
3. Darcie Sims as cited in Richard Gilbert, *Finding Your Way after Your Parent Dies* (Notre Dame, Ind.: Ava Maria Press, 1999), 11.
4. Alan D. Wolfelt, *Healing a Friend's Grieving Heart: 100 Practical Ideas for Helping Someone You Love through Loss* (Fort Collins, Colo.: Companion Press, 2001), 1.
5. Lynn Davidman, *Motherloss* (Berkeley: University of California Press, 2000), 3.
6. Leo Rosten, *Leo Rosten's Treasury of Jewish Quotations* (New York: Bantam, 1977), 332.
7. Quincy Jones, *Quincy Jones* (New York: Doubleday, 2001), 318.
8. Katherine Graham, *Personal History* (New York: Vantage, 1997), 439.
9. Ibid.
10. James MacGregory Burns and Susan Dunn, *The Three Roosevelts: Patrician Leaders Who Transformed America* (New York: Atlantic Monthly Press, 2001), 85.
11. Linda Richman, *I'd Rather Laugh: How to Be Happy Even When Life Has Other Plans for You* (New York: Warner Books, 2001), 23.
12. Arthur Ashe and Arnold Rampersad, *Days of Grace: A Memoir* (New York: Knopf, 1993), 50.
13. Ibid.
14. Russell, 54.
15. Ibid.
16. Ibid., 55.
17. Ibid.
18. Douglas H. Gresham, *Lenten Lands* (New York: Macmillian, 1988), 127.
19. Ibid., 127–28.

20. Ibid., 128.

21. Ibid., 131.

22. Jackie Joyner-Kersee, "Decisive Moment: 'I Will Never Forget What It Took to Get Where I Am,'" *The Chicago Tribune*, 18 June 1989, sec. 6, 3.

23. Edelman, vii.

24. Doug Manning, *Don't Take My Grief Away* (San Francisco: Harper & Row, 1979), 65.

25. James Robert Parish, *Rosie: Rosie O'Donnell's Biography* (New York: Carroll & Graft, 1997), 3.

26. Ibid., 4.

27. Ibid., 5.

28. Ibid., 4.

29. Ibid., 5.

30. Boyd, 39.

31. Ibid., 40.

32. Ibid.

33. Gilbert, 84.

34. Boyd, 44.

35. Collier-Slone, 3.

36. Ibid.

37. Ibid.

38. Bartocci, 50.

39. Ibid.

40. James Johnson to Harry S. Truman, 6 August 1947, Truman Presidential Library.

41. Edelman, 14.

42. Lottie Healy Jackson to Harry S. Truman, 6 August 1947, Truman Presidential Library.

43. Bill Clinton, "For Mother's Day: What I Learned from My Mother," *USA Weekend*, 6–8 May 1994, 4.

### Chapter 4: The Burying

1. Barbara Bartocci, lecture, 7 February 2001, Kansas City, Missouri.

2. Kristin Clark Taylor, *Black Women: Songs of Praise and Celebration* (New York: Doubleday, 2000), 214.

3. Bill Tammeus, "Pain Inevitably Comes into Our Lives," *The Kansas City Star*, 9 June 1996, sec. B, 7.

4. William Manchester, *Winston Spence Churchill: The Last Lion—Visions of Glory, 1974–1932* (Boston: Little, Brown, 1983), 760.

5. M. Bern-Klug, D. J. Ekerdt, and D. S. Wilkinson, "What Families Know about Funeral-Related Costs: Implications for Social Work Practice," *Health & Social Work* 24:2 (1999), 128.

6. Adam Teicher, "Andres Carries On: Loss of His Mother Latest Blow for Chief," *The Kansas City Star*, 3 August 2000, sec. D, 7.

7. Tim Dahlberg, "Nichlaus Respects Mom's Dying Wish," *The Dallas Morning News*, 17 August 2000, sec. B, 1, 13.

8. Nancy Keller, personal correspondence, 16 January 2002.

9. Ibid.

10. Frank McCourt, *'Tis: A Memoir* (New York: Scribner, 1999), 361.

11. Ibid., 362.

12. Boyd, 115.

13. Taylor, 191.

14. McCourt, 362.

15. Taylor, 205.

16. Manchester, 760.

17. Arnold Rampersad, *Jackie Robinson: A Biography* (New York: Knopf, 1997), 428.

18. Jensen, 179.

19. Barbara Bush, *Barbara Bush: A Memoir* (New York: Charles Scribner's Sons, 1994), 36.

20. David Shipman, *Judy Garland: The Secret Life of an American Legend* (New York: Hyperion, 1992), 509.

21. Taylor, 197.

22. Ellen Dissanayake, *Homo Aestheticus* (Seattle: University of Washington Press, 1995).

23. Herbert Anderson and Edward Foley, *Mighty Stories, Dangerous Ritual: Weaving Together the Human and the Divine* (San Francisco: Jossey-Bass, 1998), 118.

24. Madeleine L'Engle with Carole F. Chase, *Glimpses of Grace: Daily Thoughts and Meditations* (San Francisco: HarperSanFrancisco, 1996), 193.

25. Colin L. Powell with Joseph E. Persico, *My American Journey* (New York: Random, 1995), 301.

26. Wendy Leigh, *Liza: Born a Star* (New York: Penguin, 1993), 103.

27. Howard Clinebell, *Basic Types of Pastoral Care and Counseling: Resources for the Ministry of Healing and Growth*, rev. ed. (Nashville: Abingdon, 1984), 222.

28. Stephen E. Ambrose, *Nixon: Volume Two, The Triumph of a Politician, 1962–1972* (New York: Simon & Schuster, 1989), 128.

29. Thomas Lynch, *The Undertaking: Life Studies from the Dismal Trade* (New York: Norton, 1997), 197.

30. Lewis Grizzard, "An End to Mama's 25 Years of Pain," *The Orlando Sentinel*, 15 October 1989, sec. G, 3.

31. Timmeus, sec. B, 7.

32. James M. Wall, "Grief and Loss: A Death Observed," *The Christian Century* 114:26 (1997), 819.

33. McCourt, 367.

34. Clinebell, 222.

35. Leigh, 102.

36. Davidman, 4.

37. Christopher Andersen, *Diana's Boys: William and Harry and the Mother They Loved* (New York: William Morrow, 2001), 227.

38. Dorothy Gallagher, *How I Came into My Inheritance and Other True Stories* (New York: Random House, 2001), 21–22.

39. McCourt, 366.

40. McCourt, 367.

### Chapter 5: The Grieving

1. Andersen, 232.

2. Victoria Alexander, *Words I Never Thought to Speak: Stories of Life in the Wake of Suicide* (New York: Lexington Books, 1991), 159.

3. "Siblings Have Little Time to Grieve Death of Parents," *The Kansas City Star*, 10 June 2001, sec. A, 4.

4. Alexander Levy, *The Orphaned Child: Understanding and Coping with Grief and Change after the Death of Our Parents* (Cambridge, Mass.: Perseus Publishing, 1999), 46.

5. Alan D. Wolfelt, *Healing a Friend's Grieving Heart: 100 Practical Ideas for Helping Someone You Love through Loss* (Ft. Collins, Colo.: Companion Press, 2001), 99.

6. Nancy Keller, conversation with author, 24 March 2002.

7. Gallagher, 22.

8. Jed Johnson to Harry S. Truman, 30 July 1947, Truman Presidential Library.

9. William A. Henry III, *The Life and Legend of Jackie Gleason* (New York: Doubleday, 1992), 34.

10. Ibid.

11. Margaret Truman, *Harry S. Truman* (New York: William Morrow, 1973), 371.

12. Edmund Morris, *The Rise of T. R.* (New York: Coward, McGann & Geoghegan, 1979), 251.

13. H. W. Brands, *T. R.: The Last Romantic* (New York: Basic Books, 1997), 194.

14. Ibid.

15. Ibid.

16. Edmund Morris, *Theodore Rex* (New York: Random House, 2001).

17. Bozeman, 98.

18. Levy, 85.

19. Ibid., 46.

20. Ibid., 6–7.

21. Marc Shapiro, *Pure Goldie: The Life and Career of Goldie Hawn* (New York: Birch Lane Press/Carol Publishing Group, 1998), 165.

22. Ibid., 166.

23. Ibid., 166–67.

24. Ibid, 166.

25. Joan Delahanty Douglas, "Patterns of Change Following Parent Death in Midlife Adults," *Omega* 22, no. 2 (1990–1991), 123–37.

26. Taylor, 197.

27. Henri Troyat, *Tolstoy,* trans. Nancy Amphoux (Garden City, N.Y.: Doubleday & Company, 1967), 62.

28. Bozeman, 98.

29. James Kavanaugh in Northumbria Community, *Celtic Daily Prayer* (London: HarperCollinsReligious, 2000), 331.

30. Kirk Douglas, *My Stroke of Luck* (New York: HarperLargePrint, 2002), 14.

31. Ibid., 129.

32. Levy, 3–4.

### Chapter 6: The Remembering

1. John van Druten, "I Remember Mama" in *Three Comedies of American Family Life*, edited by Joseph Mersanded (New York: Washington Square Press, 1961), 8.

2. Alba Ambert, "Persephone's Quest at Waterloo: A Daughter's Tale" in *Lasmamis: Favorite Latino Authors Remember Their Mothers*, edited by Esmerald Santiago and Joie Davidow (New York: Knopf, 2000), 61.

3. Sally Higgins, conversation with author, 2 June 1999.

4. Michelle Windmueller, conversation with author, 24 June 2002.

5. Suzy Platt, editor. *Respectfully Quoted: A Dictionary of Quotations Requested from the Congressional Research Service* (Washington, D.C., Library of Congress, 1989), 233.

6. Benjamin P. Thomas, *Abraham Lincoln* (New York: Knopf, 1952), 58.

7. Dorothy Schneider and Carl J. Schneider, *First Ladies: A Biographical Dictionary* (New York: Checkmark Books, 2001), 164.

8. Ibid.

9. Ambert, 60.

10. Ibid.

11. Denman Dewey III, "When a Congregation Cares: Organizing Ministry to the Bereaved," *Death Studies* 12, no. 2 (1988), 123–35.

12. Thomas Attig, *The Heart of Grief: Death and the Search for Lasting Love* (New York: Oxford University Press, 2000), 27.

13. Bartocci, 55.

14. Ambert, 61.

15. Edelman, 16.

16. Dagoberto Gilb, "Mi Mommy" in *Las mamis* (New York: Alfred A. Knopf, 2000), 137.

17. Maynard, sec. C, 1.

18. Edelman, 21.

19. Ambert, 51.
20. Scott, sec. C, 5.
21. Barry Miles, *Paul McCartney: Many Years from Now* (New York: Owl/Henry Holt, 1997), 6.
22. Burns and Dunn, 86.
23. Edelman, 16.
24. *The Book of Common Prayer and Administration of the Sacraments and Other Rites and Ceremonies of the Church* (New York: Seabury Press, 1979), 267. Author's emphasis.
25. Levy, 37.
26. "Beautiful Isle of Somewhere." Text by Jesse B. Pounds, 1897.
27. "Land where we'll never grow old."
28. Nancy Keller, conversation with author, 2002.
29. Rose Marie Mansfield, conversation with author, 9 December 2001.
30. Ruth Bell Graham, "'The King Is Coming' and Other Memories of Mother," in *A Tribute to Moms*, edited by Ruth Senter and Jori Senter, (Sisters, Ore.: Multnomah Books, 1997), 89.
31. Colleen Townsend Evans, "Spring-Loaded for Fun," in *A Tribute to Moms*, edited by Ruth Senter and Jori Senter, (Sisters, Ore.: Multnomah Books, 1997), 22.
32. Higgs, 114.
33. Jensen, 179.
34. Kathy Trocolli, "Money Doesn't Grow on Trees and Other Wise Sayings from My Mother," in *A Tribute to Moms*, edited by Ruth Senter and Jori Senter, (Sisters, Ore.: Multnomah Books, 1997), 199–200.
35. Johnnetta B. Cole, "Overheard," *The Kansas City Star*, 14 March 2001, sec. F, 3.
36. Sue Bender, *Stretching Lessons: The Daring That Starts from Within* (San Francisco: HarperSanFrancisco, 2001), 91–92.
37. Miles, 6.

### Chapter 7: The Honoring

1. Jack Welch with John A. Byrne, *Straight from the Gut* (New York: Warner Books, 2001).
2. Joie Davidow, *Las Mamis,* ix.
3. Quoted in Cal Thomas, "A Dear Lady Takes Her Leave," *The Los Angeles Times*, 5 May 1997, sec. B, 5.
4. Caroline Kennedy, *The Best-Loved Poems of Jacqueline Kennedy Onassis* (New York: Hyperion, 2001).
5. Kim McMillen with Alison McMillen, *When I Loved Myself Enough* (New York: St. Martin's Press, 2001).
6. Edna P. Gurewitch, *Kindred Souls: The Friendship of Eleanor Roosevelt and David Gurewitch* (New York: St. Martin's Press, 2002).

### Conclusion

1. Sally Higgins, conversation with author, 2 June 1999.
2. Frederick Beuchner as cited in Robert Benson, *That We May Perfectly Love Thee: Preparing Our Hearts for the Eucharist* (Orleans, Mass.: Paraclete Press, 2002), 48.
3. Michelle Windmueller, conversation with author, 24 April 2002.
4. Nancy Cobb, *In Lieu of Flowers: A Conversation for the Living* (New York: Pantheon, 2000), 53.
5. Leigh, 103.

# Other Resources from Augsburg

*On Grieving the Death of a Father* by Harold Ivan Smith
144 pages, 0-8066-2714-X

By drawing from the writings of dozens of sons and daughters who have reflected upon the impact of their own fathers in their lives, Harold Ivan Smith has captured the essense of fatherhood.

*Remembering Mama* by Dara Dokas
32 pages, 0-8066-4352-8

A young girl expresses emotions connected to her loss and uses memories of her mother to work through her grief. Some of the memories are hers, others are stories people tell her about her mother. All the memories help guide her through her grief in this illustrated picture book.

*When Your Parent Dies* by Ron Klug
48 pages, 0-8066-4263-7

A brief, focused, and compassionate book that guides adults through the first days and weeks of bereavement. Drawing on his own grief experiences, the author shows how the resources of faith, family, and community can help a grieving person.

*When a Loved One Dies* by Philip W. Williams
96 pages, 0-8066-4269-6

Walk with Philip W. Williams on your journey through grief as he offers you wisdom and insight from others who have lost a loved one. He reminds the reader that God is always nearby, providing guidance, comfort, and strength.

**Available wherever books are sold.**